D0775918

BROADWAY COSTUMES ON A BUDGET

Big-Time Ideas for Amateur Producers

Janet Litherland
and
Sue McAnally

costume illustrations by
Michelle Gallardo

MERIWETHER PUBLISHING LTD.
Colorado Springs, Colorado

Meriwether Publishing Ltd., Publisher
P.O. Box 7710
Colorado Springs, CO 80933

Editor: Arthur L. Zapel
Typesetting: Sharon E. Garlock
Cover design: Tom Myers
Costume illustrations: Michelle Gallardo

Library of Congress Cataloging-in-Publication Data

Litherland, Janet.
     Broadway costumes on a budget : big time ideas for amateur
producers / by Janet Litherland and Sue McAnally. --1st ed.
        p.   cm.
     Includes bibliographical references and index.
     ISBN 1-56608-021-5 (pbk.)
     1. Musicals--Stage guides. 2. Costume. 3. Musicals--Production
and direction. 4. Amateur theater--Production and direction.
I. McAnally, Sue. 1968-   II. Title.
MT955.L58   1996
792.6'026--dc20
                                  96-1579
                                   CIP
                                   MN

1 2 3 4 5 6 7 8   99 98 97 96

ACKNOWLEDGMENT

The costumes pictured on the front and back covers
of this book were designed by Linda Johnson,
founder of Ivywild Costumes of Colorado Springs, Colorado.
Ivywild, a major costume house since 1983, serves schools,
colleges and theater groups throughout Colorado.

Contents

CHAPTER 1
Costumes Are Not Clothes

Let's Get Practical...

Every Broadway musical (and there are hundreds of them) has its own costume needs — color, movement, style, design and characterization — and every person who has ever written, designed, costumed or produced a professional musical will say that theirs is the only (or at least *best*) way to do it. Uniqueness aside, the majority of people involved with Broadway musicals today have never *been* to Broadway. They are the everyday folks who work with high school, college and community theater. They don't have big budgets, nor do they have all day every day to devote to such projects.

Costuming a Broadway musical for teenagers in Idaho, Kansas, Maine or West Virginia is much different from costuming the real thing in New York City. However, the magic of theater is such that the Kansas musical looks just as fine as the New York one — or much better — to the audience that attends and enjoys it! Their Guenevere is the most elegant Lady who ever held her head high, and their Phantom is the scariest persona who ever haunted an opera. Their costumes look terrific, didn't cost a fortune, and they weren't difficult to put together.

"But they don't look like the *real* ones!" someone sniffs.

The majority of audiences in Missouri or South Dakota or anywhere else in America doesn't know that. Nor do they care.

This doesn't mean that the amateur production has to resemble something staged by "The Little Rascals" under Granny's oak tree either. Despite its differences, high school Broadway can have all the glitz, glitter, pizzazz and panache of the "other" Broadway!

3

Crossing Over

Though the purists will always say that costumes are unique to each show, practical people know better. Most shows fall into general categories, meaning that the costumes can "cross over" and be used again and again. Many times they will need to be altered — have sleeves removed, ruffles added or trimmings changed — but flexibility is the whole point of costuming. Costumes are not made to remain forever in a perfect, unaltered state! In fact, costumes are never perfect. They're not even *clothes*! More about that later.

One hundred different musicals are listed under the following general categories. Applying the "crossover system," costumes from one show in a category can be altered for any other show within the same category. For example, the characters in *Oklahoma!* wear the same basic costumes as those in *Annie Get Your Gun*; and the teenagers in *Bye Bye Birdie* dress much the same as the teens in *Grease*. For wide variance within a category, such as *Hello, Dolly!* and *My Fair Lady* against *Oliver!* and *Les Miserables*, differences (in this case, between rich and poor) are explained in each chapter. Read on!

Medieval/Shakespearean
A Connecticut Yankee (part 1940s or contemporary)
A Funny Thing Happened on the Way to the Forum
Camelot
Kiss Me, Kate (part contemporary)
Man of La Mancha
Once Upon a Mattress
Pippin
The Boys From Syracuse
Two Gentlemen of Verona

The 19th Century/Turn-of-the-Century

Can-Can (Paris)

Carousel

Fiddler on the Roof (Russia)

Finian's Rainbow

Hello, Dolly!

Les Miserables

Maytime (operetta)

Miss Liberty

My Fair Lady

Oliver!

Show Boat

The King and I (England and Siam)

The Merry Widow (Paris, operetta)

The Music Man

The Phantom of the Opera

The Student Prince (operetta)

Western

Annie Get Your Gun (old West)

Destry Rides Again (old West)

Girl Crazy (1940s)

Oklahoma! (old West)

110 in the Shade (1960s/contemporary)

Paint Your Wagon (old West)

The Unsinkable Molly Brown (old West/Europe)

Wildcat (1912)

The 1920s

Cabaret (Germany)

Fiorello!

Funny Girl

Good News! (college setting)

Guys and Dolls

Gypsy (1920s through 1950)

Mame

No, No, Nanette

Porgy and Bess (operetta, all black cast)

Rose-Marie (Canada, operetta)

The Boy Friend

The 1930s-1940s

Ain't Misbehavin' (all black cast)

Annie

Anything Goes

Babes in Arms

Bells Are Ringing

Carmen Jones (all black cast)

42nd Street

Girl Crazy (western)

I Can Get It for You Wholesale

Jumbo (circus)

Of Thee I Sing

On the Town

Roberta (Paris)

South Pacific (military and Polynesian)

Strike Up the Band

The Sound of Music (Austria)

Where's Charley?

Wonderful Town

The 1950s-1960s

Bye Bye Birdie

Call Me Madam

Carnival

Damn Yankees (baseball setting)

Do Re Mi

Dreamgirls

Flower Drum Song (San Francisco's Chinatown)

Godspell (flower children)

Grease

How to Succeed in Business Without Really Trying

Li'l Abner (hillbilly)

Me and Juliet

Mr. President

On a Clear Day You Can See Forever

Purlie (southern, all black cast)

Stop the World — I Want to Get Off

The Fantasticks

The Pajama Game

West Side Story

Contemporary **(or can be adapted/played as contemporary)**
A Chorus Line A Connecticut Yankee (part Medieval/Shakespearean) Babes in Arms Brigadoon (part 18th-century Scotland) Carnival Damn Yankees Dancin' Girl Crazy Godspell How to Succeed in Business Without Really Trying Kiss Me, Kate (part Medieval/Shakespearean) Little Shop of Horrors Me and Juliet 110 in the Shade On a Clear Day You Can See Forever Peter Pan (part fantasy — pirates) Roberta Stop the World — I Want to Get Off The Fantasticks Where's Charley? You're a Good Man, Charlie Brown

Fantasy
Babes in Toyland (toys)
Barnum (circus characters)
Cats (talking animals)
Godspell (clown and rags, Bible theme)
Peter Pan (contemporary, fantasy characters, pirates)
The Fantasticks (surrealistic characters)
The Wiz (fantasy characters)
The Wizard of Oz (fantasy characters)
You're a Good Man, Charlie Brown (teens dressed as children)

Circus/Carnival
Carnival
Barnum
Jumbo

Costumes will not necessarily cross over within the next three categories, but it's important to know what sets the following shows apart and what makes them similar. Many of them (and their crossover possibilities) will be discussed in Chapter 9, "Myriad Periods."

Mixed Periods/Unusual Settings
A Connecticut Yankee (contemporary, Medieval/Shakespearean)
Amahl and the Night Visitors (Bible times, operetta)
Brigadoon (contemporary, 18th-century Scotland)
Dancin' (1970s)
Evita (1934-1950s South America, operetta)
Fiddler on the Roof (1905 Russia)
Joseph and the Amazing Technicolor Dreamcoat (Bible times)
Kismet (ancient Baghdad)
Kiss Me, Kate (contemporary, Medieval/Shakespearean)
Naughty Marietta (18th-century Louisiana, operetta)
South Pacific (1940s military, Polynesian)
The King and I (19th-century England, Siam)
The Merry Widow (turn of the century, operetta)
The Music Man (1912 America)
The Unsinkable Molly Brown (old West, Europe)
Timbuktu (ancient Africa)
Wildcat (western, 1912)

Operetta
Amahl and the Night Visitors
Evita
Naughty Marietta
Porgy and Bess
Rose-Marie
The Phantom of the Opera (Andrew Lloyd Webber version)
The Merry Widow
The Student Prince
(To be categorized as "operetta" for the purposes of this book, most — if not all — of the dialog is sung, rather than spoken.)

All African-American Cast
Ain't Misbehavin' (1930s)
Carmen Jones (1940s, variation of Bizet's opera *Carmen*)
Porgy and Bess (1920s)
Purlie (southern, 1960s)
Timbuktu (variation of *Kismet*)
The Wiz (variation of *The Wizard of Oz*)

The crossover system not only works between shows, it also works for a single character's scene changes, and for other characters within the same show. Here's a brief example (chapter ideas are much more detailed):

• Read the description given for the ladies' costumes in *Hello, Dolly!*.

• Keeping to the same basic styles, choose Dolly Levi's costumes, varying the colors, materials and trimmings for her different scenes.

• Dress the other ladies of *Dolly* in variations of the basic costumes, but not as opulent as those that Dolly Levi wears.

• Use the same costumes for the ladies of *My Fair Lady* and *Showboat*.

• Save Mr. Vandergelder's costumes for Mr. Brownlow of *Oliver!* and the men of *Showboat, My Fair Lady* and *The Phantom of the Opera*.

For reference, an overview of the appropriate period clothing and general suggestions for "crossing over" appear within each chapter...just to make life a little easier!

Costumes: The Essential Difference

Should costuming be a major consideration when selecting a show? In a word: No.

Costumes are not street clothes. Remember this. It's the biggest, best, most basic rule of all. Costumes are not made of fine silks and brocades, real leather or Irish lace. Nor are they constructed from designer patterns by professional tailors...they only *look* that way.

There are big differences between "clothes" and "costumes." Creating beautiful clothes can be scary and expensive. Costumes are not scary and they don't cost nearly as much as monthly payments on a Porsche! Brown velour, for example, looks like leather on stage, but costs only a fraction of the real thing. Pieces of an old curtain (donated free of charge from someone's attic) magically turn into lace.

13

Costumes should be sturdy enough not to fall apart during rigorous movement, but they don't have to be perfectly sewn. Glue, tape, and pins can be used to alter limited-use costumes. Also, non-raveling hemlines and sleeves can be cut to length and left unsewn — polyester works very well for this. Necklines and waistlines can, and should, be closed with Velcro® hook-and-loop fastening strips (or a similar product) rather than tedious snaps and buttons. Speed is essential to most costume changes; therefore, the easiest "in-and-out" method defines the best, most functional costume.

"Layering" is another quick-change technique. A character can go from rags to riches in a hurry by wearing the "rich" costume under loose-fitting rags. Quick-changes that cannot be layered will need assistance and a certain amount of privacy, both of which have to be planned.

Sometimes costumes need to be "weathered" — smudged, wrinkled, torn — so they won't look new. Real clothes would never be constructed, worn, or treated in such a way...Oops! Take that back — torn blue jeans go for big bucks in some pretty fancy department stores these days!

Shoes news: For a generation that lives in tennis shoes, energetic movement in anything else (military boots, sandals, leather dress shoes, etc.) can be a disaster. *Insist that actors rehearse in the shoes they will wear for performance.* For particularly sticky problems, comfortable ballet slippers with matching stockings can be painted to look like almost anything. They're real lifesavers — maybe literally!

Ideally, the costumer and the choreographer discuss movement problems together and find amicable, workable solutions. Example: If a particular costume — such as that of an authentic booted soldier — cannot be modified enough to allow the actor to perform an intricate dance with ease, then the dance must be modified to suit the costume. The opposite is also true: If a dance essential to a particular period — such as the 1920s Charleston — cannot be performed in the selected costume, then the costume must be modified to accommodate the dance. It's a matter of degree — the "look" may be more important in one situation and the movement in another. If costumer and choreographer cannot agree, the director makes the decision.

Rings and Things and Buttons and Bows...

Accessories can be a costumer's nightmare. They're hard to keep up with from show to show, and they present dangerous possibilities, such as broken beads, which can roll under the dancers' feet. A musical is more energetic than a play. There's more action and more opportunity for trouble. All trimmings should be attached firmly to the costumes if possible. (Think about professional ice skaters — lots of glitz and glitter, but nothing that is not nailed down!) Jewelry, particularly earrings, should be firmly secured.

Speaking of jewelry, *no personal jewelry of any kind should be worn in a show, unless it is part of the costume.* No nail polish or blue eye shadow unless the part calls for it — other eye shadows are fine, but blue shows up grotesquely under the lights. And don't allow hair to fall around the faces — acting depends a great deal on facial expression.

Back to Basics...

Costumes for the high school stage must conform to five basic rules:

1. Structured (or unstructured) so that actors can move freely and comfortably and change quickly.

2. Designed or chosen for the period (era) of the play and the age and description of each character.

3. Designed appropriately for young people to wear. (Teenagers need to feel good about their costumes. Contrary to the image they often choose to project, young folks still have an awkward streak and are easily embarrassed.)

4. Color-selected either to blend or contrast (but not clash) with the set.

5. Scaled with the size of the auditorium in mind.

"Scaling" needs a bit of explanation. Example: A subtle dress that makes a fashion statement in a *real* restaurant will make no statement at all in a *stage* restaurant of a large auditorium; however, if the stage is in a small (500 seats or fewer) theater, the subtle dress may do just fine. Define a costume's lines and color so that it may be seen and appreciated from the back row!

Not all costumes are made from scratch. Many selected pieces are given to the project or purchased for it. Clothing from the 1950s, '60s and '70s often can be found at the Salvation Army, Goodwill, and other thrift stores. It will already have the weathered look. Buttons are then removed, openings made larger and lined with Velcro® or other self-sticking strips, and hem cut to length, turning inexpensive clothes into costumes.

Borrowed clothing is another matter and is not recommended for use, since it must be returned in its original condition. This is no easy trick, even if no alterations are necessary. Hot stage lights make actors *sweat* ("perspire" is too mild a term here), particularly through a series of energetic dances, as in *Oklahoma!* or *West Side Story*. No amount of cleaning will restore the borrowed clothing, and no costume chief needs the added stress of being responsible for it.

Granted, some shows are more difficult to costume than others. To achieve the illusion of glamour for *My Fair Lady* takes more creative finagling than rounding up 1950s duds for *Grease*. Likewise, *Barnum* presents a heart-stopping challenge, while *A Chorus Line* practically costumes itself.

Even so, the costumer who remembers that his or her responsibility is to produce costumes — not perfect clothes — can gather up the courage to proceed with any show.

Spread the Fun...and the Responsibility

The costume chief is just that — a chief — not one, lonely person who must design, select, purchase, measure, cut, fit and sew all of the costumes for a cast the size of the U.S. Marine Band! The chief needs a committee of good workers with whom to share expertise.

Ideally, the committee (six to ten people) should include students who are not cast members, teachers and parents. Does the committee have to do all of the above-mentioned work? No, but it is responsible for seeing that it gets done. It is also responsible, along with the chief, for the planning process.

16

The committee's biggest problem will be sticking to the allotted budget — usually limited, sometimes nonexistent. Ideas presented throughout the following chapters will concentrate on achieving the best results at the least cost.

Parents are generally willing to help. Many, in fact, are eager because the project benefits their own children. Some help with money, some like to scout the thrift stores and attics, and others enjoy cutting out patterns and sewing. Committee members, each with assigned tasks, must enlist the parents' help.

If a singing or dancing chorus needs identical costumes (*The Music Man, A Chorus Line*, etc.), the committee might organize a cut-and-sew party in a large social hall or gymnasium. With long tables and several sewing machines, a seemingly impossible task can be accomplished in a short time and be fun, too. This is a lesson professional and experienced amateur companies learned long ago. An example: The Tallahassee (Florida) Ballet has a "costume shop" at its headquarters. This is where volunteers meet to cut, gather and sew yards and yards of net — they made seventy-six tutus for the ballet's performance of *Cinderella*.

Some costumes, not all, will be worth saving. These need to be hung in a permanent costume room, which (if the school cannot provide such a place) could be an attic or spare room in someone's home. (This co-author's [Sue McAnally] attic has been a costume room for nearly twenty years!) Keep a record of every item. If a parent has financed and constructed her own child's costume, encourage her to donate it to the costume room.

Excuse Me While I Have a Breakdown...

Sure, the costume chief has a big job! But, any self-disciplined person with a talent for organization can do it. Read that again! It's not necessary to be an artist or designer or tailor. The chief only has to *recruit* such talent and keep it in line.

In Fairfax County, Virginia, a group of fifth graders and their adult leaders have successfully adapted, performed and costumed *The Music Man, Oklahoma!, Annie Get Your Gun* and other Broadway musicals. If they can do it, high school students and their parents certainly can.

17

Remember:

• Start early — months (not weeks) in advance. A last-minute effort will look like one.

• Enlist good help and delegate responsibility.

• Keep costumes simple, yet reflective of the characters and periods portrayed. (Old bathrobes from the current century are not a costume option for the stylized *Joseph and the Amazing Technicolor Dreamcoat!*)

• Stay organized. "Lists" are the best preventive medicine for panic attack.

If you doubt your ability or stamina or courage, think of the title character in *Annie Get Your Gun*. She sings: "Anything you can do, I can do better...I can do anything better than you."

Then go do it!

CHAPTER 2
Preventive Medicine
For EVERYONE Involved in High School Productions

Give Me One Good Reason...

Why should teenagers attempt a Broadway musical? There are many good reasons. Here are four of the best:

- Builds (and in many cases *establishes*) personal confidence
- Teaches cooperation and teamwork
- Demands commitment and responsibility
- Provides a sense of accomplishment unlike any other

Consider Yourself...Informed

In the old days, Broadway musicals were for professionals. They were perceived as too extravagant, too costly, too time-consuming, too "adult," and too OVERWHELMING for high school students. Schools that did produce musicals routinely made their choices from works written especially for teenagers. The market was glutted with hillbilly comedies and whodunits. Except for a Cleaver-family-like surface sweetness, such as "boy meets girl and takes her to prom," love stories were nonexistent.

It wasn't a matter of holding Broadway musicals at bay. It was simply an assumption that they were beyond the capabilities and understanding of high school students, so why bother?

Then, in the early 1960s, teacher-directors in some of the more progressive (and more affluent) school systems began experimenting with more challenging material. Slowly and steadily over the years, Broadway musicals seeped into the programs, replacing the specially written "teen shows" as high school productions.

As with all change, this transition evoked the good, the bad, and the ugly:

• It dispelled the myth that teenagers are naive, intellectual mannequins who can only play cardboard characters — no depth or perceptive abilities.

• It turned the spotlight on a spirit of enthusiasm, teamwork and accomplishment among teens.

• Because of the cost involved, it challenged school systems and parents to support it. (Later, they discovered that such a production could generate eye-popping funds.)

• It also taught many that a lavish production can get out of control — becoming an end in itself, rather than being valuable because of the *process* of production.

• It fostered greed for bigger and better things ("Wow! How can we ever top *that*?").

• It worried adults, who were faced with the task of replacing "hells" and "damns" with more acceptable words.

• It challenged everyone to examine scenes that might be considered offensive for high school audiences.

This co-author (Janet Litherland) remembers producing and directing Broadway's *Bye Bye Birdie* for a Pennsylvania high school in the 1960s. It was the first time one had been attempted in that small city, and reaction to it ran the gamut — from elation to hostility. The production was colorful and spectacular, a moneymaker, a tremendous learning experience for the students, and it earned lengthy standing ovations both nights it played.

But there were problems. Despite careful elimination of the curse words, a hell and a damn found their way onto the stage on the final night. Teens are teens — no matter how responsible or "good" they are, they'll always try to put one toenail just over the line. Those words, which in the 1960s shocked young audiences into embarrassed giggles, incensed some adults who, naturally, blamed the director for "allowing" such words to remain in the script. Moreover, the ice-house scene drew one hostile comment in the form of a vindictive letter to the editor of the local newspaper. The scene depicts teen idol Conrad Birdie luring sweet and innocent Kim McAfee to a deserted ice house. What he wants is scarcely implied and nothing bad happens. The importance of the scene is that Kim realizes Birdie is a shallow nonperson and ceases to idolize him and his kind.

There will always be critics who pick at nits and miss the lessons. But it's important to know that they are out there and to be able to accept their barbs with a smile — without allowing your scratches to bleed! Costumers are not immune. Careless ones can find themselves on the sharp end of a barb — for outfitting young people in clothing that is too tight, too revealing, too suggestive or too avant-garde for a community's taste. This is one good reason for *not* reproducing many of Broadway's original costumes; the other, of course, is copyright infringement.

Presenting Broadway musicals in high schools is considerably easier now than it was thirty years ago. High school students and their audiences are more sophisticated, and shows like *Bye Bye Birdie* — easy to costume — are popular choices.

There are in some musicals, of course, scenes that *do* go too far and are unquestionably violent or inappropriate for high school audiences. *Man of La Mancha* and *Les Miserables* contain such scenes, yet still are worthy productions because of the inherent themes and the lessons they teach. Offensive scenes can be easily adapted or eliminated.

Tom Jones and Harvey Schmidt (writers of *The Fantasticks*) showed remarkable sensitivity to changing times when, in 1990 — the thirtieth anniversary year of their still-running show — they changed the word "rape" to "abduction" and wrote an alternative, relevant song. *Real* rape was never intended, they said. When they wrote it thirty years earlier, they intended "seize and carry off by force," a dictionary definition. Now, with victims of *real* rape having the courage to speak out against such atrocity, the world no longer thinks of the word "rape" in a literary sense. For the character El Gallo's contrived, lighthearted pursuit of Luisa, "abduction" seems a sensible alternative.

Along with the license to perform, rights are usually granted to cut portions of a show. (For licensing agencies, see Appendix B.) This is often necessary, not only because of content but also because of length. *Camelot* lasts nearly three hours, which could test the sitting power of any audience, particularly when the show is an amateur production with no major "stars." (Incidentally, the beautiful medieval costumes are a major attraction of *Camelot*.)

Which Musicals and Why...

Of the fifty shows detailed in this book, thirty-four are based on either another work — a book or play — or on the life of someone famous. These musicals had a jump-start on success, because the subject matter was already interesting to the public.

Of the originals — those conceived in imagination and thrown to chance — *Of Thee I Sing* became the first musical to win a Pulitzer Prize for Drama; *A Chorus Line* became Broadway's longest-running musical (*The Fantasticks*, mentioned earlier, is an off-Broadway show); *Finian's Rainbow, Anything Goes* and many others were smash hits of their opening seasons; and the music from *Babes in Arms* (including "My Funny Valentine") was so memorable that it is still being recorded and performed — apart from the show — nearly sixty years later!

These and others with similar histories continue to enjoy performance by both professional and amateur theater groups year after year.

All 100 shows mentioned in this book have merit. To give costumers and other workers a more complete sense of the projects they are considering, fifty of the most popular ones are described briefly, in addition to the costume notes. However, only by carefully perusing an actual script can workers determine which show is right for their group of students.

Some shows, such as *West Side Story, Les Miserables* and *Cabaret* have dark moody messages. Others are so light they seem to float on cool breezes (*You're a Good Man, Charlie Brown, Babes in Arms* and *Annie Get Your Gun*). And, *The Sound of Music, Annie* and *Oliver!* deliver serious themes on platters of pure sugar.

Still other shows, such as *Porgy and Bess* and *The Phantom of the Opera* (Andrew Lloyd Webber version), are actually operettas and require exceptional singers. If "funny" is the operative word, check out *Where's Charley?*, *A Connecticut Yankee*, *Grease* and *Anything Goes*. Patriotic themes can be found in *Mr. President* and *Of Thee I Sing*. Love stories, of course, are everywhere.

If big choruses of singers and dancers are desirable, *The Unsinkable Molly Brown, Bye Bye Birdie, Carousel, Oklahoma!* and *The Music Man* are good choices. On the other hand, if the number of available students is small, *The Boy Friend, The Fantasticks, You're a Good Man, Charlie Brown* and *A Chorus Line* would fill the bill. Too, most "big" shows (*Camelot, My Fair Lady, Brigadoon, Guys and Dolls, The King and I* and others) can be performed with a small chorus, if participants sing well. Small schools often eliminate big shows without considering the possibilities...and never know what they might have accomplished.

CHAPTER 3
Medieval/ Shakespearean

Our calendar years from 800 to 1485 are generally referred to as the Medieval Period. These were the years of peasants and nobles, kings and queens, rulers and warriors, lords and ladies, and knights in shining armor (necessary, not to save fair maidens, but to guard the settlements from constant threat of attack). Medieval years also embraced persecution and poverty, duels and dowries, and shackles and serving wenches. Times were rough, and today's musicals with medieval settings reflect that roughness.

In the early part of the period, clothing was simple but not dull. Fabrics were woven and dyed, and leather and fur were popular choices for warmth and decoration. As the period progressed, richer fabrics were developed and clothing became more elaborate, especially among the nobility. Women dressed in long, close-fitting gowns, capes and decorative headdresses; men chose knee-length tunics with long stockings and cloaks. Of necessity, the medieval poor spun and wove their own materials. Often, they twisted straw around their legs (held on with crisscrossed strips of leather) for protection.

This category is extended to include musicals based on Shakespearean themes, such as *The Boys from Syracuse* and *Two Gentlemen of Verona*, simply because the costumes cross over very well.

Medieval costumes present a challenge, but they're also fun to create. Too, actors love wearing them — these costumes *move!*

The Shows

A Connecticut Yankee, A Funny Thing Happened on the Way to the Forum, Camelot, Kiss Me, Kate, Man of La Mancha, Once Upon a Mattress, Pippin, The Boys from Syracuse, Two Gentlemen of Verona.

Authors' Crossover Choices:

A Connecticut Yankee, Camelot, Man of La Mancha, Pippin.

In the Spotlight

Pippin

Costumes for the above nine shows can be created by combining the suggestions at the beginning of this chapter, the ideas presented in "The Crossover," and the details of *Pippin's* costumes.

The Costumes

PIPPIN

Wig:	Curly blond, shoulder length.

Opening Scene

Top:	Crocheted, loose-weave sweater without sleeves in light blue or aqua (bare arms).
Trousers:	Thick, cotton-knit pants in brown, gray or dull green. (Sweat pants with elastic band cut off at ankles can be used — dye them the right color.) Use a rope belt around waist — do not tie in bow. Wrap legs (over the pants) with rust- or tan-colored strips of suede, leather, polyester or burlap (spools can be purchased from a florist or craft shop). Begin under the arch of the foot and work up, criss-crossing the strips. Tie

them just below the knee, and tuck the ends in at the top. (Briefs-type underwear should be worn with this costume, so the performer won't feel self-conscious or embarrassed.)

Feet: Bare.

Helmet: Use a lady's felt hat with brim (from a thrift store). Cut felt out in front as shown and turn brim down. Spray with silver paint and put silver brads across the cut-out portion in front. Add a purple or pink plume (from craft or fabric shop).

Costume Change

Tunic: Cut just above the knees. Full, long sleeves and belt (see Charlemagne's illustration below). Use brown tones with orange and gold trim — *less* ornate than Charlemagne's tunic.

29

Trousers: Same as above, but unwrap the legs — no strips.

Pippin as King

Add his father's cape to Pippin's costume when he becomes king.

CHARLEMAGNE *(Pippin's Father)*

Tunic: Made of velour or soft velvet-like fabric in blue or blue-gray — an over-the-head boatneck. Jewels, braid, sequins or gold and silver fabric can be glued on with fabric glue. Make a belt of

	contrasting-color fabric; add braid, and use a tasseled window-pull at the end of the braid.
Trousers:	Tan, brown or gray. Wrap legs with rust- or tan-colored strips and tuck in at top (same as Pippin's legs were wrapped).
Shoes:	Brown or tan men's closed-toe, soft vinyl house slippers.
Cape:	Use red or navy velour or an old velour blanket — something that doesn't need hemming. If not using a pattern, measure actor from back of neck to three inches from floor. Sew old fur piece or fake fur around neck. Trim with heavy gold or silver braid. Add a jeweled pin at the neck.

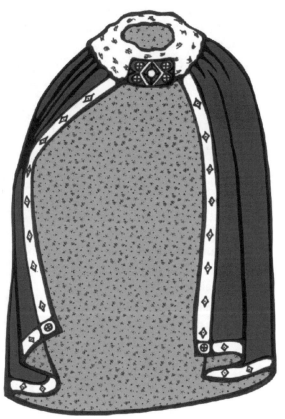

Crown: Cut poster board in the shape of a crown. Measure actor's head for fit and staple together. Spray-paint gold and add sequins or any sparkly ornaments.

BERTHE *(Pippin's Grandmother)*

Gown: Basic long tunic made of opaque material. Make the "wrap" for the skirt and the headpiece from a soft fabric — sheer polyester, chiffon, or an old curtain with original hem removed and replaced with a shirttail hem (light blue or green, if possible). Trim the wrap with gold and silver glitter and glue it to a wide belt, also trimmed. Tie the belt so it hangs, tassel-like. Trim the neckline.

Headpiece: Drape a long piece of the above soft fabric over the head, allowing it to flow across the chest. Bring lots of curled hair (or attach fake hair) up through a hole in the top of the fabric.

Shoes: Cream-colored soft shoes or house slippers. Could use slip-on tennis shoes. (If shoes are too white, dip them in a weak solution of tea.)

Accessories: Bangle bracelets and big stone rings.

DANCERS

Body: Black leotard with black tights. Plain, no-lace, black bra underneath. (Large-bosomed girls should wear underwire bra or two regular bras with tight straps to protect them from the "bouncing look" when they dance.)

Skirt: Black chiffon or nylon "handkerchief" skirts — no hem. Cut two 44" squares. Lay out, one on top of the other, to form eight points. Cut circle for waist, with placket in back. Use a sturdier

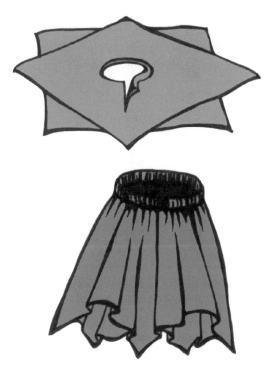

fabric for waistband. (Pretty, elastic waistbands — found in fabric shops — are available by the yard in different widths and different colors.) Measure 1½" more than waist size to allow for closure. For color, a "strip" (not striped) skirt can be added over the handkerchief skirt: Cut no-hem polyester fabric onto 2" strips and sew them to a black waistband. Strips should be the length of the longest point on the handkerchief skirt. (For bold colors choose red, blue, yellow or green; for a softer look choose mauve, gold, or lime green.)

Face: Masks are very difficult for young people to wear while performing. Clown-white faces with designs work much better. Another option is to eliminate the clown white and just add circles to the cheeks: Cut circles from colored tape and stick to waxed paper until ready for use. Attach with spirit gum — the tape will not stick by its own power throughout the performance. (Make-up circles won't do, because the heat from stage lights and the energy of the performers make it smudge. Sharp, clean lines are important here.)

The Crossover

Dress the men of *Camelot* (depending on their ages) similar to Pippin and Charlemagne. Older women will wear variations of Berthe's costume. For younger women, make the basic tunic more close-fitting; give them more elaborate headdresses — more jewels, gold braid woven through the hair, and drape and pin the chiffon in decorative arrangements; add long capes for some scenes.

Characters in *Man of La Mancha* wear medieval peasant clothing in "earth" colors: Long, blousy sleeves for both men and women; full skirts for women; full trousers tucked into high stockings at the knees for men (a rougher version of Pippin's costume); soft slippers. Use coarse materials, except for Don Quixote — dress him in gray velour pants and smooth white shirt. The Don also needs a stiff, metal-looking vest for his imagined knighthood —

make it of vinyl and spray it with silver paint. (For later repairs, look for Instant Vinyl or a similar product.)

The Don's sword can be made of ¼" plywood and sprayed with chrome paint from an auto store. Cover the handle with black electrical tape. (Note: If the group plans to enter a school competition with a knight-and-sword scene, points will be *deducted* for using a real sword.)

The knights of *Camelot* and *A Connecticut Yankee* can wear variations of Don Quixote's costume. Don't try to outfit characters in metal (or even a facsimile of metal) from head to toe, even if a script calls for it — which *Pippin's* script does. Such gear obstructs movement, and it isn't necessary. Simply create the *illusion*, such as Don Quixote's vest-only armor and Pippin's helmet.

King Arthur's basic costume is in the same style as the other men (and Don Quixote), but is made of richer material and has more trimmings. He also wears a long, decorative cape and a crown (see Charlemagne's cape and crown).

For the 20th-century characters in *A Connecticut Yankee*, see The 1920s, Chapter 6.

The Stories

Pippin

Writers:

Stephen Schwartz, Roger O. Hirson.

Comment:

The biggest hit of its season, *Pippin* is a young man's search for "self." Drama. (The ending isn't particularly uplifting; however, the individual scenes — staged *commedia dell'arte* style — are fascinating. The music has a gentle, "pop" flavor.)

Synopsis:

Through a series of vignettes, young Pippin (Charlemagne's son) explores life, turning first in one direction, then another. He tries war and love — he even tries to be an advocate for worthy causes...but nothing offers him the sense of self-worth he seeks.

This is despite (or because of) the machinations of a God-Devil character who unifies the scenes.

Weary of his search, Pippin gives up (perhaps too easily) and opts for a life of leisure.

A Connecticut Yankee

Writers:

Richard Rodgers, Lorenz Hart, Herbert Fields.

Comment:

Based on Mark Twain's *A Connecticut Yankee in King Arthur's Court.* Comedy. (For a more serious treatment of the Court, see *Camelot.*)

Synopsis:

Because he flirted with someone else, Martin's jealous fiancé bops him over the head with a bottle and sends him off to dreamland — Camelot and the "Knights of the Round Table."

In his dream, the knights (who think he is dangerous) plan to burn him at the stake. To save himself, Martin desperately recalls his history and accurately predicts an eclipse. The knights, in awe, release him. To further impress, Martin tries to modernize Camelot with telephones, radios and other 20th-century "miracles." Soon, big trouble arrives — his fiancé, in the form of Morgan Le Fay.

Mercifully, Martin wakes up (literally and figuratively) and decides to marry a different girl — the one he truly loves.

Camelot

Writers:

Alan Jay Lerner, Frederick Loewe.

Comment:

Based on T. H. White's novel, *The Once and Future King.* Drama. (The title song has since been associated with the Kennedy years: "Don't let it be forgot/That once there was a spot/For one brief shining moment that was known as Camelot." A poignant production. For a lighthearted look at Camelot, see *A Connecticut Yankee.*)

Synopsis:

King Arthur is engaged to Guenevere, but they have never met. Arthur is willing but nervous; Guenevere fears she is missing her chance for romance. Still, they marry, and Arthur is happy.

Then Lancelot (a knight) falls in love with Guenevere and courts her. When their romance is exposed, the lovers are forced to flee.

Arthur pursues them, forgives them, and purposely goes off to battle — knowing he may die, yet hoping that the flame of Camelot's "one brief shining moment" can someday be rekindled.

Man of La Mancha

Writers:

Mitch Leigh, Joe Darion, Dale Wasserman.

Comment:

Based on Cervantes' book, *Don Quixote,* and Cervantes' own life. Drama. (The show is rough, sometimes violent and always dramatic. It's about an old fool and a trollop, but audiences come away believing in a knight and his lady and "The Impossible Dream.")

Synopsis:

Crazy Don Quixote and his servant, Sancho, go where the "wild winds of fortune" blow — to a windmill, which the Don attacks, thinking it is a living giant. When he realizes what he has done, he convinces himself that a sorcerer was involved. His goal now is to become a knight so that he can destroy the sorcerer.

Always the dreamer, he chooses a poor country inn for his castle and asks the innkeeper to dub him a knight. His imaginary knighthood is soon tested when a serving wench — a trollop, whom he calls "sweet lady" — is abducted from the inn. He rescues her and, eventually, his faith changes her into the lady she never thought she could be.

Finally, in a joust with the Knight of the Mirrors, the Don recognizes himself for what he is — "a madman dressed for a masquerade" — and takes to his bed, despondent. At the end, his "lady" arrives to remind him of his noble quest for the impossible dream and to present herself as living proof of his faith.

CHAPTER 4
The Old West

Except for cowboys, men of the Old West wore the same dark, uninspired suits worn in the East (described in Chapter 5, "The 19th Century"). Likewise, western women clung to eastern fashion, but with practical modifications. Hoop skirts and layers of petticoats would have been ridiculous encumbrances on the working frontier, though such "frills and furbelows" were lovingly unpacked and worn for special, social functions.

Since frontier men and women spent many hours in the sun, brimmed hats served a practical purpose. Cowboys and cowgirls chose shirts and pants (many daring women wore trousers) in drab colors. Levi Strauss' new "jeans" were popular, first in brown, then blue. Trimmings (leather fringe, braid, silver ornaments) usually appeared on vests or gloves; chaps were made of leather or fur; and red neckerchiefs were worn for protection against dust. Boots were a source of great pride, crafted of fine leather and often "tooled" or decorated.

Historical characters who performed in traveling shows, such as Annie Oakley and Buffalo Bill *(Annie Get Your Gun)*, wore more colorful, theatrical versions of traditional clothing.

Though *Wildcat* (1912), *Girl Crazy* (1940s) and *110 in the Shade* (1960s/contemporary) are westerns, they are not of the *old* West. Costumes for these shows need to be adapted from clothing of the periods in which they are set or played.

The Shows

Oklahoma!, Annie Get Your Gun, Destry Rides Again, Paint Your Wagon, The Unsinkable Molly Brown.

Authors' Crossover Choices:

All.

In the Spotlight

Oklahoma!

Costumes for the above five shows can be created by combining the suggestions at the beginning of this chapter, the ideas presented in "The Crossover," and the details of *Oklahoma's* costumes.

The Costumes

CURLY

Shirt: Long-sleeve, western-type in a bright color. (A local square-dance group might have an old one to donate; or, check the thrift stores.) Red or blue bandanna.

Pants: Blue jeans (not faded). Brown or black belt, wider than belts worn today. If a wide belt cannot be located, wide leather belting is available by the yard in fabric shops.

Chaps: Chaps are low-slung, with a belt of their own, and are worn over the jeans. Cut them fuller than the jeans, from imitation suede. Decorate with brads and/or fringe. For fringe, cut (from scraps of the same material) a 3" piece the length of jeans and make a short slit every ½" along the piece. Or, buy imitation suede fringe by the yard from a fabric shop.

Accessories: Felt cowboy hat; cowboy boots or short pull-on boots in black or brown. Curly wears gun and holster.

LAUREY AND OTHER YOUNG WOMEN

Dresses: Simpler versions of 19th-century long dresses or blouses and skirts (see introduction to Chapter 5), made of gingham — medium or large check — in lavender, pink, orange, red or green. Cotton prints also work well. Other fabrics to choose from are polished cotton, cotton polyester and organdy.

Aprons: Long aprons, worn while doing chores. Muslin or gray cotton.

Hats: Hats are pretty, but more functional than those worn in the East (as seen in *Hello, Dolly!*, Chapter 5). Western hats are brimmed for a purpose — to shade the sun. Worn in some scenes by some of the young women.

LAUREY'S WEDDING ENSEMBLE

Dress: Choose any white fabric that has a sheen: polished cotton, chintz, satin; and white lace to trim the high neck and wrists. Begin with long

white skirt and sash. Make a fitted bodice with long sleeves (full at shoulders and fitted at wrists — see illustration for Aunt Eller's dress, page 46). Drape the hip area with matching fabric, an old white lace tablecloth or curtain, or a piece of dotted swiss. Drape is similar to Berthe's in *Pippin* (see illustration, Chapter 3), except Laurey's drape fastens in back. Attach the drape to zipper seam in back and pin on a big bow where the ends of the drape meet. Make a bow 8"-12" wide and doubled from dress fabric, and use iron-on interfacing between the doubling to give the bow some body. It should be long enough to drop somewhat (not stand up straight). Long, full slip under gown.

Headpiece: Cut a piece of lace (old tablecloth) 36"-44" wide and 36"-45" long. Tuck one side under the front edge of a cloth-covered, white metal headband and sew in place. Let the remaining lace flow down the sides over the ears. Add a small white circle of flowers on top of the head, using bobby pins to hold it in place.

Shoes: White flat shoes or low-heeled pumps without trim.

NOTE: Jean's wedding dress (*Brigadoon*, Chapter 9) can be modified for Laurey by adding some fullness to skirt and sleeves.

AUNT ELLER *(and variations for older ladies)*

Dress: Long dress or skirt and blouse of cotton or cotton polyester. Choose beige or cream background with small designs or flowers in the fabric. Bodice has a high neck with full sleeves that taper to the wrists. Make belt in a color from the design in the fabric — a remnant works fine. Cut it 4" longer than the girl's waist and 4" wide (doubled) and use iron-on interfacing to give it body; add a skirt hook-and-eye in the back (no bow). Put a beige, brown or light gray shawl around her shoulders.

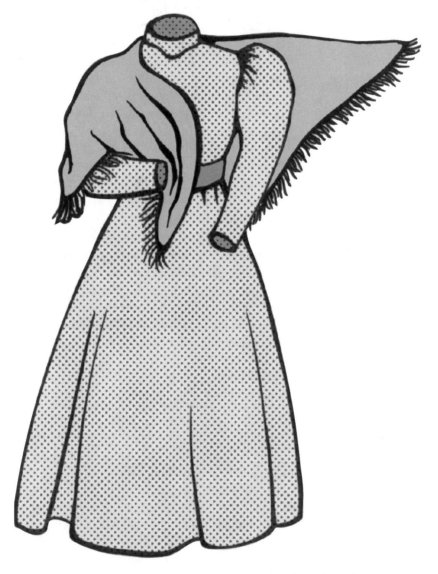

Petticoat: If an old, red, long full skirt is available, use it as a slip under the dress. If not, purchase the least expensive red fabric possible and make a drawstring top by folding the fabric over about an inch, sewing it down, and running cord or ribbon through the resulting tubular pocket. (This can be used for all sizes of waists and needs no hemming.)

Hat: Choose a flat shape in black, brown or beige. Attach a ribbon on each side, which can be pulled down to tie under the chin. Put a coordinating flower on top.

Shoes: Black, oxford-type shoes with black stockings.

Drawstring
Bag: Make a paper pattern by drawing a 16" circle (use a large round platter or bowl for quick circles). Cut the circle from a remnant of velour, velvet, brocade or satin. Draw another circle (this time on the cloth) about 2½" inside the rim. Sew two pieces of bias tape (both sides) around the inner circle, without joining the pieces — so that a long cord can be pulled through as shown.

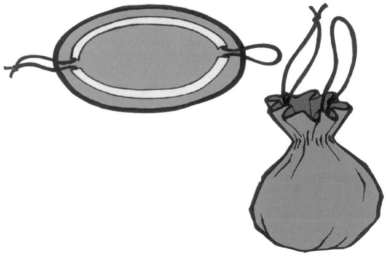

Parasol: A parasol can be used in different scenes for Aunt Eller and some of the other ladies. Choose a small umbrella in a solid color.

The Crossover

Costumes from *Oklahoma!* will work very nicely for *Paint Your Wagon, Destry Rides Again* and the western scenes in *The Unsinkable Molly Brown*. For *Molly's* European scenes choose clothing from *Hello, Dolly!* (Chapter 5). The character "Destry" needs a suit, preferably plaid or checked — see Chapter 5 for style.

Oklahoma's costumes will also work for most of the characters in *Annie Get Your Gun*, but some will need a little more of the "cowboy" look (see beginning of this chapter). The show-within-a-show characters (Annie, Frank and Buffalo Bill) need flashier costumes — brighter colors, more trimmings — because they are "performers." For them, be generous with brads, fringe and silver ornaments.

The character "Frenchy" in *Destry Rides Again* will need a cutaway dress, since the shy Destry accidentally (and with great embarrassment) tears part of it off. Cut a piece out of the skirt, from mid-thigh to hem on one side and reattach it with Velcro strips. A ruffle along one side of the cutaway will give Destry something to grab onto.

Laurey's wedding dress *(Oklahoma!)*, with a few modifications, will do very nicely for Jean in *Brigadoon* (Chapter 9).

The Stories

Oklahoma!

Writers:

Richard Rodgers, Oscar Hammerstein.

Comment:

Based on Lynn Riggs' play, *Green Grow the Lilacs*. Musical play. (Because it was not an original work, *Oklahoma!* was not eligible for a Pulitzer prize; however, it was given a special award by the Pulitzer committee. This show's songs and dances enhance, rather than interrupt, the story line. Plenty of action.)

Synopsis:

A young man, Curly, arrives at Aunt Eller's farm to court Laurey, his "on-again, off-again" love. After a quarrel, Laurey accepts an invitation from Jud Fry to attend a box social. Curly asks another girl, but warns Jud to leave Laurey alone.

In a dream, Laurey realizes she is afraid of Jud. At the social, Curly and Jud try to outbid each other for Laurey's box supper and Curly wins. Jud, however, dances with Laurey and threatens her just before he leaves the party. When Curly comforts her, she realizes she truly loves him.

At their wedding, Jud appears with a knife, fights with Curly and is killed. With the wedding guests as jury, a local judge acquits Curly and the wedding proceeds. The couple ride away in a "surrey with the fringe on top."

In a side story, which necessarily relieves dramatic tension throughout the show, Ado Annie and Will Parker walk a rocky (and comic) road to romance.

Annie Get Your Gun

Writers:

Irving Berlin, Herbert Fields, Dorothy Fields.

Comment:

Based on the true-life, 1890s story of Annie Oakley. Comedy. (Ethel Merman was the original Annie. Her song, "There's No Business Like Show Business" became a musical theater classic.)

Sypnosis:

Annie Oakley is a country girl with a lively personality and a talent for sharpshooting. To support her family, she joins Buffalo Bill's Wild West Show and becomes its star. Her costar is Frank Butler.

Annie falls in love with Frank, but Frank is uncomfortable with her superior marksmanship. They argue (in song), "Anything you can do, I can do better!" Annie doesn't realize that this is not the way to win Frank.

It is Chief Sitting Bull who persuades her to lose a match to Frank. She does, and romance blossoms. (The idea of deliberately losing may not please the "politically correct" thinkers of the 1990s, but it makes great entertainment!)

Destry Rides Again

Writers:

Harold Rome, Leonard Gershe.

Comment:

Comedy. Stage adaptation of a popular film. (Flashy choreography is what makes this show work — lots of movement and color. This is an old-fashioned "good guys vs. bad guys" story, and the good guys win.)

Synopsis:

The town fathers of Bottleneck (a frontier town) hire Thomas Jefferson Destry, Jr., as sheriff. His mission is to send the noisy, disruptive "Kent Gang" packing so the town can reclaim itself. Trouble is, Destry is shy and doesn't believe in violence. He tries to settle the problems lawfully, but he is comically unsuccessful and is finally forced into a shootout. Destry wins the battle (of course!) and turns the town into a peaceful haven. He also wins the girl, Frenchy. She was part of the Kent Gang, but she admired Destry and decided to change her ways.

Paint Your Wagon

Writers:

Alan Jay Lerner, Frederick Loewe.

Comment:

Comedy-Drama. Depicts the life and death of a town during the gold rush. (A rich, rollicking musical peppered with authentic events — lots of fun to perform. Memorable songs: "I Talk to the Trees" and "They Call the Wind Mariah.")

Synopsis:

When gold is discovered on Ben Rumson's land, a "boom town" rises and becomes prosperous.

Ben's daughter, Jennifer, is in love with Julio Valveras, a miner. Ben, however (with his newfound wealth), has bigger and better plans for his daughter and sends her away to school and away from Julio.

When the gold is depleted, the town dies and so does Ben. Jennifer returns, and she and Julio resume their romance. Together, they make plans to turn the town into an irrigated farming community.

The Unsinkable Molly Brown

Writers:

Meredith Willson, Richard Morris.

Comment:

Based on the life of the real Molly Brown, whose activities gained notoriety from the turn of the century to 1912. (Big dance numbers, marches, and singing choruses.)

Synopsis:

Molly is a poor, Missouri girl with visions of grandeur and the imagination and energy to turn them into reality. She moves to Colorado and falls in love with Johnny Brown, a miner. They marry and take Johnny's "claim" money (a small fortune) to Denver, where they attempt to settle among wealthy citizens.

Snubbed, they go to Europe, where they become socially popular. Returning to Denver for revenge, Molly gives a big party but is embarrassed when Johnny's old mining buddies show up. Molly and Johnny separate, and she goes back to Europe.

After a time, Molly realizes that she still loves and misses Johnny and decides to return to him aboard the *Titanic*. When the ship sinks, Molly survives and becomes a heroine through her efforts to help others. Because of her heroism, she wins back her husband and gains acceptance into society.

CHAPTER 5
The 19th Century/ Turn-of-the-Century

French and English fashions dictated clothing styles during the 19th Century.

Men wore somber suits with vests, topcoats, top hats and bowlers. Hair was plastered down with perfumed oil (rural men used bear grease), and various styles of moustaches were considered handsome. Like men of today, they wore their "fashion accents" around their necks — cravats, scarves, long ties and bow ties. Men didn't make many changes during this period.

Women's fashion, however, was as fickle as adolescent love. First they wanted the simplicity of the "Grecian" look — a muslin sheath laced just under the bosom, shawls and classic hair styles. Two decades later they wanted the opposite — billowing, ballooning skirts and sleeves, and hairdos that would make a giant oak tree weep!

Through the remainder of the century, women experimented with: skirts and blouses (a new idea); large, feathered and flowered hats; petticoats, hoops and pantalets; long, straight skirts with bunchy bustles; tassels, fringe, beads and bows; modest high-necks and gaping low-necks; and, through most of it...tight corsets, which no doubt accounted for the ladies' frequent attacks of "vapors"!

In the last decade, clothing became more functional and less experimental. Throughout the century, the poor (as in *Oliver!* and *Les Miserables*) didn't worry about fashion. They wore either drab homespun or layers (for warmth) of threadbare, ill-fitting cast-offs, their trimmings long since removed.

The Shows

Can-Can, Carousel, Finian's Rainbow, Hello, Dolly!, Les Miserables, Maytime, Miss Liberty, My Fair Lady, Oliver!, Show Boat, The Phantom of the Opera, The Student Prince.

Authors' Crossover Choices:

Carousel, Finian's Rainbow, Hello, Dolly!, Les Miserables, My Fair Lady, Oliver! Show Boat, The Phantom of the Opera.

In the Spotlight

Hello, Dolly!

Costumes for the above twelve shows can be created by combining the suggestions at the beginning of this chapter, the ideas presented in "The Crossover," and the details of *Hello, Dolly's* costumes.

The Costumes

THE LADIES *(including Dolly)*

Blouse: High collar; full sleeves, puffed at shoulders (see also bodice illustration for Aunt Eller, Chapter 4).

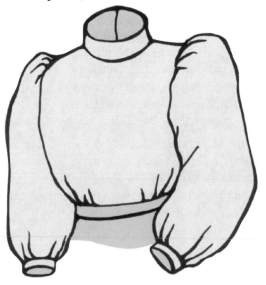

Skirt: A-line, longer in back (like a "train," but not as long). Matinee-length — just above the ankles, so performers won't trip during movement. An old chiffon or organdy prom gown can be used as a skirt — put blouse over the gown and tuck ends behind the wide belt, which comes down to a point in front and buckles in back. Add a bustle (attach a *small* pillow to the underslip, using safety pins).

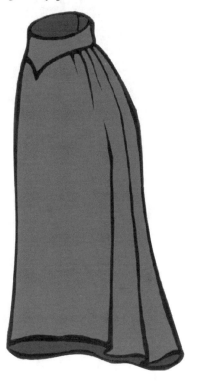

Jacket: Short and buttoned in front. Can be made from a short suit jacket — take in the waist at the back of jacket for a "fitted" look.

Hat: A felt or stiff fabric "picture hat" with flowers, feathers, stuffed white doves or other birds (Christmas-bird ornaments work great) and lots of tulle (for decoration and/or to tie under the chin). Smaller hat (straw) can have a big tulle bow in back, be decorated on top, and be anchored to the hair with a hat pin.

Accessories:	Short white gloves; drawstring bag of taffeta, velvet or velour (see Chapter 5 for directions); brooch, cameo, rope beads, watch on a pin or a chain; full, ruffled long slip; high-top laced boots; or plain low-heel pumps with black or white tights (19th-century legs were always covered).
Dolly's parasol:	Add a same-color ruffle to a solid-color umbrella. Use 2" satin or taffeta ribbon, twice the length of the circumference of the umbrella. Sew a loose-stitch line lengthwise down the middle of the ribbon. Pull one thread tighter to gather into ruffle, then sew to the umbrella.

MR. VANDERGELDER

Suit:	Purchase a gray or brown three-piece suit at a thrift store. Sew contrasting braid around the collar and lapels, down one side of coat front, along entire bottom, and across top of pocket. Vest may be plain or striped.

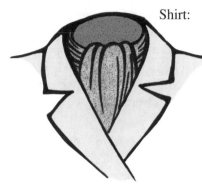

Shirt: Cut the collar off an old dress shirt and put an ascot in its place; or, round off the collar points and use a string tie.

Accessories: Bowler hat and short-top boots that either zip or pull on.

The Crossover

Use variations of the ladies' materials, colors and trimmings for the ladies of *Showboat, My Fair Lady* and *The Phantom of the Opera*. Dress the men of those shows in variations of Mr. Vandergelder's costume — choose different colors, different styles of shirts, and omit the braid on some of the suits.

Eliza Doolittle *(My Fair Lady)*, in early scenes, wears a hand-me-down version of the ladies' dresses above — weathered, smudged and minus the trimmings. Julie *(Showboat)* wears more vibrant colors, such as scarlet or emerald, a shawl, and black mesh stockings.

The ladies of *Carousel* and *Finian's Rainbow* wear simpler versions of the same clothing — minus the jackets, hats and gloves — in pastel colors. Dress the character Finian like Mr. Vandergelder, but in shades of green. Add a plaid vest and a flat, plaid "tam-o-shanter" hat, which has a small pompom on top. Sometimes Finian will wear a kilt (which will cross over into *Brigadoon*, Chapter 9). Og, the leprechaun, needs pointy ears and a green felt hat with a feather sticking up. Tuck his britches into the tops of knee-length argyle socks in shades of green. For the other men in these two shows, see *Brigadoon*, Chapter 9.

Mr. Brownlow of *Oliver!* will also dress like Mr. Vandergelder.

For the other men (and boys) of *Oliver!* and *Les Mis*, see both *Brigadoon* and *Fiddler on the Roof*, Chapter 9. Women in these shows can dress in variations of Golde's costume *(Fiddler)*.

The *Phantom* (of the Opera) needs a mask: Easiest solution is a plastic Halloween mask that fits snugly over the face and is secured by an elastic band around the head. Cut the mask so that it covers both eyes and one side of the face — nostrils are exposed. Paint the mask white.

Costumes from *Hello, Dolly!* will also cross over into *The Music Man*, Chapter 9.

The Stories

Hello, Dolly!

Writers:

Jerry Herman, Michael Stewart.

Comment:

Based on Thornton Wilder's *The Matchmaker*. Comedy. (Set in 1890s New York, this show presents a challenge in high-style scenery, costumes and staging.)

Synopsis:

Dolly Levi is a professional matchmaker. As such, she presents two women to wealthy Horace Vandergelder for his consideration, while secretly planning to snag him for herself. On the side, she helps Horace's daughter romance a young man of whom her father does not approve.

Dolly arranges for Horace and one of the possible "matches" to meet in a Manhattan restaurant. By chance, the second woman also shows up — in the company of Horace's shop assistant. This causes instant problems. So, too, does Dolly, who makes a grand entrance and shifts Horace's attention to herself.

When the entertainment begins, Horace discovers that his daughter is in the chorus of singers and her young man is a soloist. Rather than blustering, Horace smiles, admitting to himself and the others that Dolly is the woman of his dreams.

Carousel

Writers:

Richard Rodgers, Oscar Hammerstein.

Comment:

Based on Ferenc Molnar's play, *Liliom*. Called a "musical play." (Incorporates fantasy, is deeply dramatic and filled with heart-wrenching moments. Voted "Best Musical of 1944-1945" by the New York Drama Critics' Circle.)

Synopsis:

Billy Bigelow, a hard-shelled carnival barker, falls in love with Julie Jordan. As he courts her, his hard shell cracks, revealing a shy young man. Julie, too, falls in love and they are married.

When Billy learns that a child is on the way, he worries that he won't be able to support his family. This leaves the door open for his old buddy, Jigger, to entice him into unsavory solutions. They stage a robbery, but when Billy knows he will be caught, he kills himself.

Switching to fantasy, the action shifts to purgatory, where Billy begs for another chance and gets it: He can return to earth and redeem himself by helping his daughter, who is now a young lady graduating from school.

Again, Billy makes a mess of things on earth and is whisked back to purgatory — but not before he sees determination and faith in the faces of his wife and child. He is assured they have a good future without him, that they will "never walk alone."

Finian's Rainbow

Writer:

Burton Lane, E. Y. "Yip" Harburg, Fred Saidy.

Comment:

Irish fantasy. (This smash hit is filled with tongue-in-cheek political and social comments. Delightful, singable music.)

Synopsis:

With a pot of gold stolen from the leprechauns in Ireland,

Finian McLonergan arrives in Rainbow Valley, Missitucky. He plans to plant his gold at Fort Knox and watch it grow. With him is his daughter, Sharon, and a leprechaun (Og) who followed them.

Sharon falls in love with Will, an American, and Og falls in love with Sharon. Love is further complicated by the social environment of 19th-century southern America — segregation and prejudice — and Sharon, making a wish, inadvertently turns a white senator black! She is saved by Og's magic, which restores the man's original color and also gives speech to Susan, a girl who is mute. When Og realizes he cannot have Sharon, he easily falls for Susan.

Sharon plans to stay in Missitucky with Will. Finally, Finian admits that his pot of gold is imaginary. But what does it matter? True riches are found in love and in friendships, not in gold!

Les Miserables (Les Mis)

Writers:

Claude-Michel Schonberg, Alain Boublil, Herbert Kretzmer.

Comment:

Based on Victor Hugo's novel. Billed as an "event" rather than a musical. (This is a strong drama that moves audiences to tears. Adult situations may not be acceptable in many schools; however, the novel is included on the school curriculum in several countries.)

Synopsis:

Think of this story as a 19th-century version of television's and film's *The Fugitive*. (Actually, *The Fugitive* was loosely based on *Les Mis*.)

Jean Valjean is a convict who is pursued throughout his life by Javert, an obsessed lawman. But the message of this musical is much more than that. It is a condemnation of social injustice and a plea for everyone to try to make the world a better place. It is a collection of miserable characters who act and interact under a three-spoke religious umbrella: Belief in the Old Testament God of wrath and vengeance; stubborn faith in the New Testament God of love and redemption; and existence, day to day, with no God at all.

My Fair Lady

Writers:

Alan Jay Lerner, Frederick Loewe.

Comment:

Based on George Bernard Shaw's *Pygmalion*. (Winner of the Drama Critics' Award and the "Tony," *My Fair Lady* set a new standard for musicals — to be a cohesive entity, rather than fragmented episodes of singing and dancing.)

Synopsis:

Professor Henry Higgins (a "phoneticist") and his colleague, Colonel Pickering, exit the opera house to find dirty flower seller Eliza Doolittle hawking her wares. Her abominable speech patterns interest them. "Why can't the English teach their children how to speak?"

Higgins remarks that he could take a mud-smudged waif, such as Eliza, and turn her into a lady. After they leave, Eliza dreams of such a transformation and sings, "Wouldn't It Be Loverly?" Excited by the idea, she shows up on Higgins' doorstep. He is at first appalled, then challenged.

After a lengthy struggle as teachers, Higgins and Pickering finally take Eliza out in public, where (to their horror) she makes crude statements in perfect English.

Ultimately, the transformation is successful and the men congratulate each other, ignoring Eliza. Angry and disillusioned, she returns to her old neighborhood, where she is no longer recognized nor accepted.

Higgins, meantime, has "grown accustomed to her face." As he sits in his study, sadly reminiscing, Eliza quietly returns.

Oliver!

Writer:

Lionel Bart.

Comment:

Based on Charles Dickens' *Oliver Twist*. Comedy-drama. (*Oliver!* has a touching and appealing flavor.)

Synopsis:

Oliver is an orphan who is banished from the workhouse because he asked for more food. On his own in the world, he joins a band of young pickpockets led by the kindly (if not misguided) Fagin. Eventually, he is rescued from a life of crime by wealthy old Mr. Brownlow, who conveniently turns out to be his grandfather. Memorable songs: "Food, Glorious Food" and "Consider Yourself."

Showboat

Writers:

Jerome Kern, Oscar Hammerstein.

Comment:

Based on a novel by Edna Ferber. The first "musical play" — a story about real people, rather than an operetta or musical comedy. (Spans forty years, giving characters an opportunity to "age" on stage.)

Synopsis:

In 1880, the *Cotton Blossom*, a showboat filled with traveling players, docks in Mississippi. During the stay, Cap'n Andy's daughter, Magnolia, falls in love with Ravenal, a riverboat gambler; and player Julie LaVerne, a sultry songstress, falls for a showboat worker named Steve.

Julie's dreams are shattered when the sheriff arrives, charging her and Steve with miscegenation — Steve is white and Julie has Negro blood. Rather than cause problems, they leave the ship. Ravenal assumes Steve's duties, and he and Magnolia marry.

In 1893, Magnolia and Ravenal visit the Chicago World's Fair. They are still in love, but Ravenal's secret gambling has put him in enormous debt. Riddled with guilt, he deserts Magnolia and their daughter.

Magnolia stays in Chicago and applies for a job to replace an alcoholic singer, who turns out to be Julie LaVerne. Magnolia doesn't recognize her; but Julie, recognizing Magnolia, gives up the job without a struggle and walks out — so that Magnolia can support her child. After a short, unhappy time, Magnolia returns to the *Cotton Blossom*.

In 1920, when Magnolia's daughter is grown, an old man approaches the showboat. He is Ravenal, still in love with Magnolia, who is also old. Loving him, too, she invites him back into her life.

The Phantom of the Opera (Three versions)

Writers:

Andrew Lloyd Webber *or*

Arthur Kopit and Maury Yeston *or*

Joseph Robinette and Robert Chauls.

Comment:

Based on Gaston Leroux's novel of the same name, *Phantom* had previously been a film starring Lon Chaney. (Spectacular sets — from the grand staircase of the opera house to the dark, misty Paris sewers — can be as entertaining as the actors and music.)

Synopsis:

A disfigured, masked madman haunts the Paris opera and kidnaps Christine, a young chorus girl. The "phantom" (whom everyone believes is a ghost) sends the worried cast a note saying "the angel of mercy has her under his wings" and that Christine must be given the lead role in the opera.

A terrified Christine returns to the stage and to her boyfriend, Raoul, who asks her to marry him. When Christine accepts, the phantom becomes very angry and curses them.

During rehearsal, the phantom appears on stage and frightens everyone, capturing Christine once again and unmasking himself. Christine tells him that the true distortion isn't in his face but in his soul.

Raoul, begging for Christine's freedom, ends up with the phantom's rope around his own neck. To gain Raoul's freedom, Christine conceals her terror and kisses the phantom, who then drops the rope, enabling Christine and Raoul to run off together.

As an angry mob approaches, the phantom wraps his cloak around himself and disappears.

NOTE: Since the Andrew Lloyd Webber version is still running on Broadway, the rights for amateur production are not yet available.

The Kopit-Yeston version has received much critical acclaim. ("This wonderful adaptation...has glory all its own." — *The Boston Globe;* "The music is simply gorgeous." — *Theatre Week*; "One of the most appealing American musicals of recent years." — *Dallas Morning News).*

The Robinette-Chauls version is easy to perform and to produce and is well within the range of most groups.

All three versions are based on Leroux's novel. For licensing information on each, see Appendix B.

65

CHAPTER 6
The 1920s

The Jazz (or Flapper) Age ushered in radical fashion changes. Women's skirts crept up to the knee for day wear and slithered down to midcalf for evening. The straight, shapeless look was "in" — no waist, no bust, no head...well, almost none. Hair was cut very short and worn under cloche (close-fitting) hats, because a small head was considered smart. Equally smart was the flappers' posture — the "Slouch." Another, very different, 1920s look was a fitted two-piece dress with a long straight skirt.

Fabrics were lightweight and pleats were popular, as were T-strap shoes and envelope purses. Women of this era loved bright colors, dangling fur pieces and "bangles" (costume jewelry), and were the first to wear colored nail polish.

Men, too, were increasingly informal. Jackets were shorter, shoulders sharper, pants wider, and belts replaced suspenders. Stripes and checks were popular, knickers were sporty and spats were spiffy. Men's hair was shorter and, except for pencil-thin moustaches, facial hair all but disappeared. (The "hair" men liked to wear was on their backs — in bulky raccoon coats!) Men also enjoyed trench coats and hats and used fancy umbrellas as walking sticks.

The Shows

Cabaret, Fiorello!, Funny Girl, Good News!, Guys and Dolls, Gypsy, Mame, No, No, Nanette, Porgy and Bess, Rose-Marie, The Boy Friend.

Authors' Crossover Choices:

Cabaret, Fiorello!, Funny Girl, Guys and Dolls, Gypsy, Mame, Porgy and Bess, The Boy Friend.

In the Spotlight
Guys and Dolls

Costumes for the above eleven shows can be created by combining the suggestions at the beginning of this chapter, the ideas presented in "The Crossover," and the details of *Guys and Dolls'* costumes.

The Costumes

SKY MASTERSON

Overcoat: Made from yellow or lime green cotton fleece fabric or an old velour blanket.

Suit: Black and white stripe; white shirt; black and white polka-dot tie or solid black.

Hat: Man's brimmed felt hat, spray painted yellow or lime green to match overcoat.

Shoes: Black and white (the kind with laces).

(Most of these items can be found in thrift stores.)

SISTER SARAH BROWN *(Of the Save-A-Soul Mission)*

Suit: Navy blue. Trim the collar and sleeves with red grosgrain ribbon. Skirt should be 3"-4" below the knee; blouse is white with high neck.

Cape: Navy blue. Should be longer than suit jacket, but not as long as the suit skirt. Tie it at the neck with ribbon or use Velcro fastener.

Hat: Bonnet-type hat in navy blue. Make from a pattern, using cotton, cotton polyester, polyester or gabardine.

Shoes: Oxford-type tie shoes in navy or black; navy or black opaque tights for the legs.

(Check thrift stores for above items.)

THE GUYS

Zoot Suits: Double-breasted, oversized suits in stripes, plaids and bright colors. (Thrift stores will have them.) Wear with vest and a carnation in the lapel. Some possible combinations: **Pink plaid suit** — turquoise shirt, pink tie, pink shoes. **Navy-and-white-stripe suit** — navy shirt, white tie, navy shoes. **Yellow and black suit** — yellow shirt, black tie, black shoes. **Maroon suit** — pink shirt, maroon tie, brown shoes. **Raspberry-and-white-stripe suit** — raspberry shirt, white tie, black and white shoes. **White or off-white three-piece suit** — black shirt, white tie, black and white shoes. That's the idea. Dye the shirts and spray paint the shoes.

Hats: Brimmed, felt hats (like Sky's) — but only for *some* of the men.

THE DOLLS

Dresses: Made from satin or fabric with a sheen. V-neck or sweetheart neckline; long straight skirts, hems well below the knees.

Jumpsuit: Long sleeves, straight legs; neckline same as for dresses. If jumpsuit has a pocket on the bodice, add handkerchief for color.

Shoes: Platform soles; high heels with strap across the instep (such as a black dance shoe) or T-straps.

Accessories: Flowers in the hair; clip-on earrings; short gloves.

The Crossover

If the colors are toned down, men's costumes from *Guys and Dolls* work perfectly for *Fiorello!, Gypsy, Funny Girl, The Boy Friend,* and the early scenes in *Mame*. (*Mame* moves from the 1920s through 1946, so check Chapter 7 [The 1930s-1940s] for the sequence of costumes as the characters age.) The men of *Cabaret* wear the same basic styles, but in much more somber colors.

Women in *Fiorello!, Mame* (in the 1920s), and *Gypsy* need variations of the "dolls' " dress and/or jumpsuit. In *Cabaret*, Sally's street clothes and clothes of other women also would be comprised of variations on the dolls', except that the colors should be less dramatic; fewer trimmings.

Gypsy's Baby June (and the older June, who pretends to be "Baby" June) can wear Bo Peep's dress (*Babes in Toyland,* Chapter 10) minus the bloomers and bonnet. Dress her hair in sausage curls and put a matching bow on top.

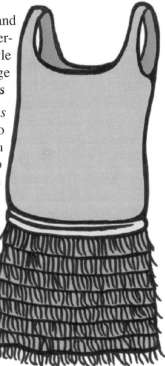

For women in *The Boy Friend* and *Funny Girl,* and Sally's outfits for entertaining in *Cabaret,* choose flapper-style dresses — shapeless and short — fringe trim, strings of beads and bangle bracelets

The characters of *Porgy and Bess* have neither the money nor the heart to follow fashion trends. Dress them in loose, comfortable clothes — use drab colors. A *quick* dip in gray or brown dye will "drab" the materials — even dipped in the same dye, no two materials will come out the same color. Some of the women in this show wear old, lace-up boots.

Costumes from *Fiddler on the Roof* (Chapter 9) can cross over into *Porgy and Bess.*

The Stories

Guys and Dolls

Writers:

Frank Loesser, Jo Swerling, Abe Burrows.

Comment:

Based on Damon Runyan characters. Comedy. (Offers an entertaining peek at New York's scruffiest inhabitants during the 1920s.)

Synopsis:

Nathan Detroit runs a crap game, but the police know about him. If he could just come up with $1,000, he could rent the Biltmore garage and have the "oldest established permanent floating crap game in New York."

Nathan particularly wants to attract a high-better named Sky Masterson. When he and Sky meet, they discuss girls and Sky brags that he can get any girl he wants. Nathan bets him ($1,000, of course) that he can't, and Sky accepts the challenge.

Just then the "Save-A-Soul Mission Band" marches by and Nathan points to Sister Sarah, the leader. Sky gulps, but gives it a try. He even bribes her with the promise of delivering "one dozen genuine sinners" to the mission if she will join him for dinner. Sarah refuses him, but later, when her superior threatens to close the mission for poor attendance, she accepts Sky's offer.

After a magnificent date, twelve gamblers are pointed toward the mission. Nathan loses his $1,000 bet with Sky, but the experience forces him to acknowledge his feelings for Adelaide, to whom he has been engaged for fourteen years. Nathan reforms and marries Adelaide, and Sky (very much reformed, in a Mission uniform) marries Sarah.

Cabaret

Writers:

John Kander, Fred Ebb, Joe Masteroff.

Comment:

Based on the play, *I Am a Camera*, by John van Druten, which was taken from Christopher Isherwood's collection of *Berlin Stories*. Drama. (Made into an Academy award-winning movie. Depicts the rough life in Berlin during the 1920s. Subject matter may be perceived by some as too grim.)

Synopsis:

Cliff Bradshaw, a young American writer en route to Berlin, meets Ernst Ludwig, a friendly young German who asks Cliff to help him smuggle some money through customs. Cliff is amused and helps.

In Berlin, Cliff finds a room in a boarding house and a girlfriend (Sally) in a nearby cabaret — the Kit Kat Klub, a gaudy reflection of a decaying society. He is happy, or thinks he is, until Ernst appears and wants help with more smuggling. It soon becomes clear that Ernst is a Nazi and is aiding the cause.

When a rock is thrown through the boarding house window, Cliff begs Sally to leave Germany with him. Instead, she returns to the cabaret and he follows her. There, he argues with Ernst and is badly beaten.

When Cliff discovers that Sally (who continues to sing "life is a cabaret, old chum,") has had an abortion, he leaves her. In the last scene, Cliff is alone on the train, remembering, and writing it all down.

(Songs sung at the cabaret serve as commentaries on the show's plot.)

Fiorello!

Writers:

Jerry Bock, Sheldon Harnick, George Abbott, Jerome Weidman.

Comment:

Based on the events leading to Fiorello La Guardia's campaign for mayor of New York City in the 1920s. Satire. (Awarded a Pulitzer prize in 1959.)

Synopsis:

The curtain opens on Fiorello reading comics to children during a newspaper strike. His followers believe he is "On the Side of the Angels."

When Thea, leader of the strike, is arrested on a false charge, Fiorello takes on corruption. He then runs for district office against the Tammany candidate. His appeal to the people is so great that the "boys" at the poker club, who half-heartedly supported him, are amazed to find that "The Bum Won."

Fiorello falls in love, goes to war, returns, and falls in love again before launching his successful campaign for mayor.

Funny Girl

Writers:

Jule Styne, Bob Merrill, Isobel Lennart.

Comment:

Based on the life of comedienne Fanny Brice, star of the *Ziegfeld Follies*. (Barbra Streisand originated the role. Her recording of "People" became a hit before the show opened and is still popular today. Big production numbers, opulent costumes.)

Synopsis:

This true story opens in Fanny's dressing room. She is waiting, nervously, for a reunion with her husband, Nicky Arnstein, who has been in prison for embezzlement.

From here, the show becomes a series of "flashbacks," as Fanny reminisces about her past: her first audition; first job as a singer; meeting Nicky; joining *Ziegfeld's Follies* and touring; marrying Nicky and financially backing his casino; Nicky's losses of both money and pride, and his arrest.

In the final scene, Nicky arrives at the dressing room. He and Fanny still love each other, but both realize that their marriage will never be truly happy. He leaves, and Fanny vows that nothing will ever again get in the way of her career.

Gypsy

Writers:

Jule Styne, Stephen Sondheim, Arthur Laurents.

Comment:

Based on the life of Gypsy Rose Lee. A true musical play, written in the style of musical comedy — dance routines, choruses, love songs. (Requires two sets of actors for the parts of June, Louise and the Newsboys — first as children, then as young adults.)

Synopsis:

Rose is the ultimate stage mother, pushy and overbearing. She is determined that her beautiful daughter, "Baby June," will become a STAR. She uses her other daughter, Louise, as background material and treats her that way, too.

At a vaudeville house, Rose meets Herbie, a candy seller. They like each other instantly, and Herbie becomes the girls' agent. However, times are hard during the depression, and there's never enough money to go around.

Before long, June elopes with a young man. Her mother is furious. Suddenly, Rose remembers her other daughter and begins turning all her energy and visions of stardom toward Louise. Unfortunately, it's too late for vaudeville (which is dead) and prim Louise is forced into burlesque.

When she realizes that the family's survival is up to her, Louise inches out of her shell and performs with a spectacular, understated style previously unknown in burlesque. Her success as "Gypsy Rose Lee" is nothing short of phenomenal.

In the end, Rose, suffering a breakdown, realizes that the stardom she craved for her daughters was actually for herself.

Mame

Writers:

Jerry Herman, Jerome Lawrence, Robert E. Lee.

Comment:

Based on Patrick Dennis' novel, *Auntie Mame*, which had already been produced as a play and a movie. Comedy. (Story begins in the 1920s and ends in 1946.)

Synopsis:

A spirited, well-to-do Mame finds herself in charge of her orphaned young nephew, Patrick. She is dotingly permissive, comic and inept, until the stock market crashes in 1929, leaving her penniless. Undaunted, she lands a part in a musical comedy, where she ruins the intended romantic effect of swinging from a moon on stage. Her next job, as a manicurist, nets her a rich Southern gentleman, whom she quickly (and fondly) marries so that she can resume her life of luxury.

As years pass, Mame's husband dies, and Patrick grows up. Mame now has time on her hands and uses it to meddle in Patrick's affairs, making shambles of his various romances. When Patrick finally marries and has a son, Mame picks up her old habit of spoiling a child in hilarious ways.

One day she questions whether she is an "old" woman. Her best friend replies, "Not old, merely somewhere between forty and death!"

Porgy and Bess

Writers:

George Gershwin, DuBose Heyward, Ira Gershwin.

Comment:

Based on Heyward's novel, *Porgy*. Folk opera; all-black cast. (Because of the intense drama and difficult music, *Porgy and Bess* requires exceptional actors and singers.)

Synopsis:

As a baby falls asleep to the songs of its parents on a hot summer evening, the southern Catfish Row slum where they live comes alive. It is a dangerous place — drinking, gambling, stealing, and even murder.

Porgy, who is crippled, gets around in a cart. He is in love with

Bess, a murderer's girlfriend. When Crown (the murderer) goes into hiding, Porgy pursues Bess, who returns his affection. However, Crown reappears, fights with Porgy, and is killed by his own knife.

Porgy is taken to jail for the crime. Persuaded that he will never be released, Bess goes to New York with a druggie named Sportin' Life. But Porgy *is* released and joyously brings a new dress home for Bess. When he finds her gone, he is brokenhearted.

Not one to give up easily, Porgy convinces himself that he can find Bess and make everything right again. Singing "I'm on My Way," he heads for New York…in his cart.

The Boy Friend

Writer:

Sandy Wilson.

Comment:

A stylized spoof of the 1920s. Charming and funny. (Displays perfectly the exaggerations and clichés of the times, including the "Charleston" dance. Fortunately, the fun of this show is not dependent on the plot, which is intentionally shallow — another angle on the spoof. Small cast functions as a large chorus.)

Synopsis:

Boy meets girl; boy loses girl; boy gets girl; boy and girl live happily ever after. (Sounds like a romance novel!)

Tony (of noble birth) falls in love with Polly (an English heiress) while posing as a delivery boy.

Polly is (of course) instantly attracted to Tony. Thinking he is poor, she pretends also to be poor so that he will love her.

Separated (naturally) by misunderstanding, they are reunited (as in "fate") at the Carnival Ball, where they arrive (coincidentally) dressed as Pierrette and Pierrot. Finally, they acknowledge their love for each other with truth. (Who could ask for anything more?)

CHAPTER 7
The 1930s-1940s

A great variety of styles reflected the vacillating moods of women during this turbulent twenty-year period. Influenced by film siren Mae West, women gave up the "slouch" of the 1920s to show off bosoms and waistlines. Hems settled in at midcalf.

These were the days of short gloves, Peter Pan collars, "beads," lots of buttons, and mother-and-daughter dresses. Bows and scarves were popular accessories, and hair was worn longer and curled. To show off the new hair styles, going hatless suddenly became chic, though some women still clung to flat straw hats, large felt ones, and turbans. Nylon stockings were instantly popular, but production was curtailed during and after World War II.

Wartime made all cloth and dyes scarce, forcing men into lighter colors, plainer patterns, and softer construction. Men also began to wear lower-cut dress shoes and embraced a new style — loafers! They still enjoyed hats, especially straw "Panamas" (straw was an abundant commodity) and flat-top caps.

Just as women were influenced by Mae West, young men were influenced by Clark Gable. After seeing the film star's state of undress in *It Happened One Night,* they abandoned their undershirts!

During the 1940s, women adopted a more militaristic look — square-cut padded shoulders, wide collars and yokes, and straight-cut slacks. They also struggled to maneuver on high wedge heels and platform soles.

Mothers liked to see their little girls in full-skirted dresses with puffed sleeves and sashes; flat shoes and tights to match. Some girls wore fitted vests over their dresses; some wore pinafores. Mothers also chose knickers and stockings with oxford-type shoes, and little suits and shirts with Peter Pan collars and ribbon ties for their little boys.

The Shows

Ain't Misbehavin', Annie, Anything Goes, Babes in Arms, Bells Are Ringing, Carmen Jones, 42nd Street, Girl Crazy, I Can Get It for You Wholesale, Of Thee I Sing, On the Town, Roberta, South Pacific, Strike Up the Band, The Sound of Music, Where's Charley?, Wonderful Town.

Authors' Crossover Choices:

Annie, Anything Goes, Babes in Arms, Bells Are Ringing, Of Thee I Sing, South Pacific, The Sound of Music, Where's Charley?.

In the Spotlight

South Pacific

Costumes for the above seventeen shows can be created by combining the suggestions at the beginning of this chapter, the ideas presented in "The Crossover," and the details of *South Pacific's* costumes.

The Costumes

NELLIE FORBUSH

(Before she "washes that man right out of her hair")

Top:	Dark-colored halter top with plenty of material in it (Not a skimpy 1990s swimsuit top!).
Bottom:	Blue jeans or navy blue pants rolled up just below the knee. Legs should be loose-fitting. Bare feet.
Coverup:	(Worn after she washes her hair) Sew two towels together as shown, leaving openings for arms and neck. Cut down through the middle of one towel, so that it can be worn like a coat. Make a soft belt from fabric that matches the towels and wrap it around the waist, tying in front.

Shorts:	White or tan, fitted at waist and hips, but full at thighs. No pockets, or very small pockets.
Blouse:	Coral, green or pink. Fitted, with short sleeves. Tie shirttails together at the waist in front.
Gown:	A sundress bodice with long, full circular skirt in green, pink or coral. Put layer of thin, white chiffon over the skirt and let the pretty color beneath show through.
Shoes:	Plain, medium-heel pumps.

EMILE DE BECQUE

Shirt:	Khaki work shirt with short sleeves or rolled-up long sleeves ("safari" type, which fits over the trousers and is belted at the waist). Brown belt.

Pants: Khaki or light brown cotton — work pants will do nicely.

Shoes: Brown riding (tight-fitting) boots.

Formal wear: White dinner jacket; white tuxedo shirt; black bow tie; black trousers; black socks; and black shoes that lace.

(Check with an Army-Navy store for the khakis; also for Luther's hat.)

LUTHER BILLIS

Shirt: Old, faded denim. (Paint a tatoo on the front of Luther's torso.)

Pants: Navy blue cotton pants, rolled up.

Shoes: Work boots that tie; no socks.

Hat: Round, white sailor hat.

Funny
costume: Purchase a grass skirt at a costume shop — swimming trunks are worn underneath. Make his "bra" from a coconut shell: Saw the shell in half. Drill two holes in each side of each shell and one hole in the top of each shell. Lace them together with string, cord or thin rope as shown. Tie in back and around the neck. Feet are bare, but there is a band of flowers around one ankle — sew artificial flowers to a piece of elastic.

The Crossover

In *South Pacific*, Emile's khaki outfit, minus the belt, will do for Lieutenant Cable. With the belt, it will suit the aviator in *Babes in Arms* and will give a simple, though not authentic, uniform look to the soldiers in *The Sound of Music* — add swastika emblems. Another easy, more "spiffy," uniform look can be achieved by trimming old, dark blue suits with black braid and epaulets. Belt the suit coat and add a piece of black belting across the chest — attach to regular belt on one side of the front, draw up and over the opposite shoulder and down to attach to belt in back.

The sailors in *Anything Goes* (and the *South Pacific* sailors who entertain) wear Luther's hat, plus white bell-bottomed pants and white pullover shirts trimmed with navy blue braid around the neck and sleeves; also a navy scarf is worn around the neck, tied low in front (like Boy Scouts tie theirs); black shoes. An alternative is white T-shirts with the white bell-bottoms.

For other military personnel, or for a more authentic look, check with an Army-Navy store.

For the characters in *Of Thee I Sing, Anything Goes* (other than sailors), *Where's Charley?, Bells Are Ringing, The Sound of Music* (except for soldiers and nuns), *Babes in Arms, Annie*, and all children, implement the suggestions at the beginning of this chapter.

Nuns in *The Sound of Music* wear black habits. Begin with a basic tunic (see illustration for Berthe — *Pippin,* Chapter 3). Slip a white, mock-turtleneck dickey in at the neckline. Add a black cloth belt, tied at one side, and attach a large cross (about 4" long) to one end. Cross can be made of cardboard and painted silver. Encircle the face, covering hair and ears, with a wide white sweatband. Attach a long piece of black material to a headband (see directions for Laurey's wedding headpiece — *Oklahoma!,* Chapter 5) and put it over the head to meet the back edge of the sweatband. Allow material to hang loosely over the shoulders and down the back.

The Stories

South Pacific

Writers:

Richard Rodgers, Oscar Hammerstein, Joshua Logan.

Comment:

Based on two of James A. Michener's *Tales of the South Pacific*. Drama. (Simply and elegantly put together, with no formal choreography. Winner of the Pulitzer prize for drama, a Drama Critics' Award for Best Musical, and a Tony Award — best in every category.)

Synopsis:

It was wartime (World War II) on an island in the South Pacific.

Emile de Becque, a French planter who lives on the island, loves Nellie Forbush, a spunky Navy nurse. An American lieutenant, Joe Cable, is in love with Liat, a Polynesian girl. Both romances are tainted with prejudicial feelings — Nellie says she cannot marry de Becque because he is the father of two Polynesian children; and Cable cannot marry Liat because of her race.

84

Then, Cable is assigned to establish a secret base behind enemy lines. He convinces de Becque (whose vast knowledge of the island will be an asset) to assist him. Unfortunately, it is a mission from which only de Becque returns. Nellie's arms, however, now welcome him, as she has come to terms with her prejudice.

Annie

Writers:

Charles Strouse, Martin Charmin.

Comment:

Based on the comic strip, "Little Orphan Annie." (In addition to major characters, the show requires a small group of children and a dog. An imaginative musical that takes liberties with history.)

Synopsis:

Annie escapes from an orphanage (and from the clutches of its mean-spirited matron, Miss Hannigan) to search for her parents and ends up with Daddy Warbucks, a wonderful, wealthy old man.

Her life with Warbucks is exciting. She gets to meet President Franklin D. Roosevelt and also J. Edgar Hoover, who helps her look for her real parents.

When it is determined that her parents are deceased, Warbucks tries to adopt Annie, but mean Miss Hannigan manages to block his efforts temporarily. Eventually, the adoption goes through and Annie, like Cinderella, lives "happily ever after."

Anything Goes

Writers:

Cole Porter, Guy Bolton, P. G. Wodehouse, Howard Lindsay, Russel Crouse.

Comment:

Comedy. (Showcases a group of odd characters — similar to the "Gilligan's Island" bunch — on an ocean liner.)

Synopsis:

Reno Sweeny is a female singer, formerly an evangelist.

Moon-Face is a gangster posing as a clergyman.

Billy Crocker is a stowaway, who is following his girlfriend.

Hope Harcourt (Billy's girlfriend) is a debutante, who is unhappily sailing to meet her future husband, Sir Evelyn Oakleigh, for a marriage of convenience.

To hide his presence on the ship, yet still get to be with Hope, Billy adopts a succession of hilarious disguises.

Fortunately, Hope learns (just in time) that she has suddenly come into money — she is rich and has no need to marry Oakleigh. So, she runs off with Billy, leaving the proper Sir Evelyn with wild Reno Sweeny.

Moon-Face provides comic interludes.

Babes in Arms

Writers:

Richard Rodgers, Lorenz Hart.

Comment:

Happy show with a happy ending. (Show-within-a-show format offers young performers an opportunity to display their own talents. Bright, memorable songs, including "My Funny Valentine," remain popular.)

Synopsis:

To raise money, which will keep them from being sent to a work farm, a group of young teens present a talent show. Unfortunately, their show is a failure — the money raised is no more than a pittance — and they are taken away. When they befriend a French aviator who makes an emergency landing in a nearby field, they are rescued. This attracts so much publicity that the teens are able to restage their show, attracting a sellout crowd. With this windfall, they build their own youth center — a much better place than the work farm!

Bells Are Ringing

Writers:

Jule Styne, Betty Comden, Adolph Green.

Comment:

Comedy. (Set in the late 1940s, when telephone services were gaining popularity — *a la* "ringy-dingy." Songs, "Just in Time" and "The Party's Over" remain popular standards today.)

Synopsis:

Ella Peterson works for an answering service called "Susanswerphone." She is a sweet, cheerful, naive girl who gets herself into big trouble by eavesdropping on her customers' conversations and involving herself (comically, however well-intentioned) in their lives.

One of her customers, Jeff Moss, is a young playwright. Ella "helps" him by persuading him to rewrite his play based on a producer's comments, which she overheard. Ella and Jeff fall in love.

Ella's real troubles begin when she helps another customer, Sandor, by taking orders for "records." Actually, Sandor is a bookie and Ella (unknowingly) is taking bets — three dozen Beethoven's Fifth is third horse, fifth race, Belmont! When Ella is exposed by the police, Jeff is disillusioned and their romance seems to be over.

The inevitable happy ending, however, has Jeff returning "Just in Time," as a much wiser Ella leaves the city for good.

Of Thee I Sing

Writers:

George Gershwin, Ira Gershwin, George S. Kaufman, Morrie Ryskind.

Comment:

Comedy. The first musical to win a Pulitzer prize for drama. (Hilarious satire. Makes fun of every aspect of American politics.)

Synopsis:

The story centers around the campaign of John P. Wintergreen for President.

After much searching for a platform, Wintergreen and his bumbling advisors decide to run on "love." Problem is, the unmarried Wintergreen has no one at home to love, so his cronies decide to have a beauty contest to select "Mrs. Prexy."

Who's the vice-presidential candidate? No one can remember. It's uh...oh, yes, Alexander Throttlebottom, whose mother is ashamed that her son might become Vice President.

Diana Devereaux wins the beauty contest, but Wintergreen would rather have the secretary, Mary Turner, who can bake corn muffins. He chooses Mary, and everyone sings, "Love Is Sweeping the Countryside." But not for long.

Diana Devereaux protests and so does France, whose ambassador deems Miss Devereaux's dishonor an insult to his country. Meantime, Wintergreen has married Mary and become President, and What's-His-Name has become Vice President. The mumblings of "dishonor" and "insult" become mumblings of impeachment, which grow into hideous (and hilarious) reality.

As Vice President, Throttlebottom must preside over the impeachment, but no one can remember who he is or where he is. When Throttlebottom finally appears, Wintergreen announces he is stepping down — his wife has given birth to twins, and he must stay home to help with them.

Who gets to be President? Throttlebottom, of course. He also gets — happily, but with a sharp stab of fear — the beautiful Miss Devereaux.

The Sound of Music

Writers:

Richard Rodgers, Oscar Hammerstein, Howard Lindsay, Russel Crouse.

Comment:

Based on the autobiography of Maria Von Trapp, *The Trapp Family Singers*. (Despite its heavy storyline — escaping from the Nazis — this is a "sweet" musical. Critic Walter Kerr wrote, "...not only too sweet for words but almost too sweet for music." This is a show that audiences absolutely *love!*)

Synopsis:

In 1938, in an Austrian convent, a young postulant, Maria, is told she is not yet ready for convent life. She is too free-spirited — she loves to sing and run and play. So, Mother Abbess sends her to care for the seven children of Captain Georg Von Trapp, a widower who treats his children as miniature military personnel.

Maria's teaching methods are much softer than the Captain's, and much more fun — especially the songs she teaches them — and the children quickly attach themselves to her.

Though the Captain is engaged to a beautiful, wealthy woman, he and Maria can't help falling in love. They marry and, for a short time, their large family enjoys an amateur sort of celebrity as the "Trapp Family Singers."

Unfortunately, the Nazis invade Austria, and the Trapp family is forced to flee. Together, they cross the Alps into Switzerland, where they will be safe.

Where's Charley?

Writers:

Frank Loesser, George Abbott.

Comment:

Based on Brandon Thomas's play, *Charley's Aunt*. Comedy. (Innocent fun without innuendo.)

Synopsis:

Two Oxford University students, Charley and Jack, decide to entertain two very proper young ladies in their rooms. They must have a chaperon, of course, so Charley agrees to play the part of his own aunt, coming and going in and out of disguise. Two problems appear — the girls' guardian, who takes a liking to "Charley's aunt"; and Charley's real aunt, who suddenly shows up. The most engaging and enduring song of this show is Charley's rendition of "Once in Love With Amy."

CHAPTER 8
The 1950s-1960s

Dior's "New Look" of the 1940s (full bust, tiny waist and gathered skirt) carried nicely into the 1950s, where women added crinolines and batwing sleeves. Another look — fitted dress with "boat" neck — was equally popular, particularly with short jackets and pillbox hats.

Any woman of the 1990s who remembers attending the 1950s or '60s prom will remember the full, strapless evening gown made of nylon net. She will also remember the painful, fashion foible that sent her, forty years later, to the podiatrist — high-heeled shoes with pointy toes! No wonder she enjoyed loafers and saddle shoes with bobby socks when she wasn't dressed up! She also sought escape from physical restriction in the shapeless, voluminous muumuu.

"The man in the gray flannel suit" was more reality than fiction during this period. Various shades and textures of black and gray stuck to men throughout the 1950s. Suit shapes were slimmer and more natural looking — an Ivy League influence — and vests were back in style. Colors returned in the 1960s, along with lightweight sweaters, slacks and loafers.

Just as women abandoned hats in the previous two decades, men said no to them in the '50s and '60s, despite the desperate attempts of hat makers to earn a living.

Other trends: Poodle skirts and ponytails, bubble skirts, miniskirts with boots, bell-bottomed pants, leisure suits, turtlenecks and Nehru jackets. And don't forget the "big hair" enjoyed by women in the 1960s — bouffants, teased and sprayed into all kinds of shapes, including fans and beehives!

The Shows

Bye Bye Birdie, Call Me Madam, Carnival, Damn Yankees, Do Re Mi, Dreamgirls, Flower Drum Song, Godspell, Grease, How to

Succeed in Business Without Really Trying, Li'l Abner, Me and Juliet, Mr. President, On a Clear Day You Can See Forever, Purlie, Stop the World — I Want to Get Off, The Pajama Game, West Side Story.

Authors' Crossover Choices:

Bye Bye Birdie, Call Me Madam, Grease, Mr. President, West Side Story.

In the Spotlight

Grease

Costumes for the above eighteen shows can be created by combining the suggestions at the beginning of this chapter, the ideas presented in "The Crossover," and the details of *Grease's* costumes.

The Costumes

GIRLS

Pants Outfits: Straight jeans (no pleats or "baggies"), rolled up to just below the knees. Jeans roll up easier if a couple of inches have been cut off the bottom. "Pedal pushers" (midcalf tapered slacks) also are a great '50s look.

Girls wear men's white dress shirts (no button-down collars), which can be found at thrift shops. Tie at the waist or leave shirttail out. Scarves of different colors are tied around the neck.

White jazz shoes are best for dance numbers, but inexpensive, white canvas tennis shoes (oxford style) will also work. Saddle oxfords and penny loafers look great on those who are not dancing. White bobbysocks are worn with the shoes. It looks best if all girls wear the same kind of socks — purchase a six-pack (or more) at a discount store.

Hair is worn in high ponytail with bow or scarf. (No gold or silver barrettes, because they reflect stage lights.)

Skirts Outfits: Long circular skirts (about 3" above the ankle) and "Poodle" skirts (plain circular skirt decorated with a big cut-out of a poodle — yep, they really wore 'em). Also, straight skirts reaching well below the knees and worn with a wide belt.

Cardigan sweaters worn with Peter Pan collars, or with pointed collars turned up in back; also cardigans worn backwards and buttoned down the back, with sleeves pushed up (add Peter Pan collars or scarves). Some of the girls can wear short-sleeved, jewel-neck sweaters.

Prom Gowns: Formal gowns of the 1950s were made of net, chiffon and taffeta. Lots of fullness in the skirt. Ruffles-from-waist-to-hemline is very much a '50s look. Length is midcalf or to the floor.

SANDY DUMBROWSKI

Since Sandy is more conservative than the other girls, she can wear a shirtwaist dress with belt and cardigan sweater in the same color. Her hair is in a ponytail with a same-color ribbon.

THE PINK LADIES

Give them straight skirts with blouses or sweaters. Their pink, "club" jackets (worn with sleeves rolled up) set them apart. This is one case (jackets) where borrowing may be a necessity, and many hospitals' "Pink Ladies" (volunteers) have exactly what's needed. Take good care of the jackets and have them professionally cleaned before returning them.

The Pink Ladies of *Grease* need bubblegum.

BOYS

Shirts: White T-shirts with sleeves rolled up to the shoulders. Black leather jackets, jeans jackets, and/or sweaters bearing the school letters.

Pants: Jeans, but not too tight. Worn with a black or brown, thin leather belt (not the "rope" type).

Shoes:	Saddle oxfords, penny loafers, or high-top tennis shoes.
Hair:	Slicked back with gel or mousse.
Accessories:	Pencil behind one ear; tattoos (such as "MOM") made with a black pen; a comb in pocket to use from time to time.

DANNY ZUKO

Black jeans, black T-shirt with rolled-up sleeves and a black leather jacket. White socks and black loafers. Danny's hair is slicked back, but with a curl in the middle of his forehead.

The Crossover

The '50s teen-wear of *Grease* is perfect for the many teenagers in *Bye Bye Birdie*. Conrad Birdie himself is just a big kid. Give him bell-bottomed pants and silky shirts in light colors — he wears his collars turned up in back. For a serio-comic effect, dress the *Birdie* cast in choir robes for the song, "Hymn for a Sunday Evening (Ed Sullivan)."

The teenagers of *West Side Story* dress similarly, but their clothes are weathered and not nearly as fashionable. Use darker shades of red, green and blue. To separate the Jets from the Sharks, give the members of each gang some kind of identifying symbol — same jackets or shirts, or same tattoos, etc.

For adults in all of these shows (including *Call Me Madam* and *Mr. President*), follow the suggestions at the beginning of this chapter.

The Stories

Grease

Writers:

Jim Jacobs, Warren Casey.

Comment:

Comedy. (Makes fun of 1950s fads — boys' slicked hair and

girls' bouffants, tight jeans, rock-and-roll music, jitterbug dances, pajama parties and more. Plot is almost nonexistent, which should leave young audiences thinking: There's got to be more to life than just "hanging out.")

Synopsis:

A group of young adults gathers for a high school reunion and relives their bebop days — growing up in the 1950s, when kids had "nowhere to go" and "nothing to do." These kids didn't really form gangs — they were more like clusters: the Burger Palace Boys and the Pink Ladies.

Danny Zuko (a "greaser") and Sandy Dumbrowski (sweet and innocent) are attracted to each other, though Sandy doesn't fit into Danny's crowd very well. Each tries to persuade the other to change.

Sandy thinks she can't compare to the flashy Betty Rizzo, leader of the Pink Ladies, and laments that she's a "poor man's Sandra Dee."

Suddenly, she decides to show them all — she makes up her face, poofs her hair and sings a swinging version of "Look at Me, I'm Sandra Dee," a song Rizzo had sung earlier with nowhere near as much pizzazz.

The show ends with everyone getting along just dandy.

Bye Bye Birdie

Writers:

Charles Strouse, Lee Adams, Michael Stewart.

Comment:

Comedy. The first musical to acknowledge "rock and roll." (Spoofs the effect Elvis Presley had been having on teenagers.)

Synopsis:

Conrad Birdie is the singing sensation whose musical gyrations enthrall the teenagers of Sweet Apple, Ohio, and upset their very conservative parents.

As a publicity stunt, Conrad's agent and his secretary have

arranged for "One Last Kiss" to be sung to a Sweet Apple girl on the Ed Sullivan Show before Conrad is drafted into the Army.

Kim McAfee is selected, making her boyfriend jealous and nearly giving her father a stroke.

In the end, Kim recognizes Conrad's shallow nature for what it is and returns to Hugo, her boyfriend.

A funny side plot involves a romance between the agent (Albert) and the secretary (Rose), and the meddlesome antics of Albert's mother.

Call Me Madam

Writers:

Irving Berlin, Howard Lindsay, Russel Crouse.

Comment:

A "take" on President Truman's appointment of Perle Mesta as ambassador to Luxembourg. Comedy. (Spoofs politics, foreign affairs, and efforts of the not-so-worldly-wise American abroad.)

Synopsis:

Sally Adams has been appointed ambassador to Lichtenburg because she is "The Hostess With the Mostess on the Ball." She is definitely an undiplomatic diplomat, but this is the very trait that somehow charms Lichtenburg's Prime Minister.

Too, Sally's assistant, Kenneth Gibson, is pursuing Lichtenburg's Princess Maria. Both couples are falling in love, but there are opposing forces at work. "Sebastian Sebastian" and his cronies want Sally ousted.

Eventually, the opposition succeeds, but not until both love stories reach happy conclusions.

Mr. President

Writers:

Irving Berlin, Howard Lindsay, Russel Crouse.

Comment:

Comedy. (This was Irving Berlin's last musical. Contains elements reminiscent of the Trumans, Eisenhowers and Kennedys. A real flag-waver!)

Synopsis:

The curtain opens on a huge White House party, where stiff-necked guests are (horrors!) dancing the "Twist." When the President and First Lady appear, everyone suddenly "waltzes" — until the prestigious couple leaves, then they break into the Twist once again.

Because of a humiliating, bad decision involving protocol with a foreign power, the President loses his next election. However, because he truly loves his country (He sings "This Is a Great Country"), he returns to a position in government at the request of the new President.

West Side Story

Writers:

Leonard Bernstein, Stephen Sondheim, Arthur Laurents.

Comment:

A 1950s version of Shakespeare's Romeo and Juliet. Drama. (This powerful show converts the family feuds of the Montagues and Capulets to gang wars between Puerto Ricans and "other Americans." In this version, Juliet [Maria] does not die, though Romeo [Tony] does.)

Synopsis:

Tony, former leader of a street gang called the Jets, and Maria, whose brother leads the rival Puerto Rican Sharks, are in love. They try very hard to keep peace, but a gang fight (rumble) is inevitable. The Jets challenge the Sharks and excitement builds.

When the rumble finally begins, Tony tries to break it up and ends up killing Maria's brother. Even so, Maria still loves Tony, though her friends urge her to stay away from him.

Then, Tony is killed by one of the Sharks. Finally ashamed of themselves, the gangs join together to remove Tony's body. Maria is left grieving.

CHAPTER 9
Myriad Periods

Some shows either do not fit into a specific period or setting, such as *The King and I* (set in 19th-century England and Siam); or the period and/or setting is unique enough that the show cannot be grouped with others, such as *Fiddler on the Roof* (1905 Russia).

Still, these shows are immensely popular and deserve attention. *The Music Man* (1912 America) opened on Broadway in 1957 — it is still a solid hit with all age groups.

Many of the costumes for such unusual offerings can be adapted from other periods. Some, such as the costumes in *Joseph and the Amazing Technicolor Dreamcoat*, require a little research before giving them their "stylized" look.

Menotti's *Amahl and the Night Visitors* is not a Broadway show, but it is a lovely little Christmas opera, well within the capabilities of high school students, provided they sing well. Use the Bible-times costumes described under *Joseph and the Amazing Technicolor Dreamcoat* in this chapter, but play them straight — don't "stylize" them as required for *Joseph*.

Dancin' is a 1970s piece that requires a whole lot of what the title promises. So, if your group doesn't sing particularly well but loves to MOVE, go for this one!

The Shows

Amahl and the Night Visitors, Brigadoon, Dancin', Evita, Fiddler on the Roof, Joseph and the Amazing Technicolor Dreamcoat, Kismet, Naughty Marietta, 110 in the Shade, The Merry Widow, The King and I, The Music Man, Timbuktu, Wildcat, You're a Good Man, Charlie Brown.

Authors' Crossover Choices:

Brigadoon, Fiddler on the Roof, Joseph and the Amazing

Technicolor Dreamcoat, The King and I, The Music Man, You're a Good Man, Charlie Brown.

In the Spotlight

All six of the authors' choices are discussed below — the shows and their costumes. The finished productions will be worth every bit of the costuming challenge they present!

Brigadoon *(Contemporary and 18th-century Scotland)*

Written by Alan Jay Lerner and Frederick Loewe, *Brigadoon* mixes fantasy and reality.

Two contemporary American hunters lose their way in a murky Scottish forest. They are drawn to a quaint village called Brigadoon, where a celebration is in progress. The young men join in, making friends with oddly dressed villagers, who refuse to accept American money and have never heard of telephones!

It seems that Brigadoon is a village caught in time, existing for only one day every hundred years. The problem: If even one villager leaves, Brigadoon will vanish forever.

The two young men return to modern-day New York but cannot forget Brigadoon or the two young women of whom they had grown especially fond.

Eventually, they go back to Scotland, hoping they can make Brigadoon reappear. Strangely, it does. The reason: "When ye love someone deeply, anythin' is possible." The young men elect to remain in Brigadoon.

Costumes for *Brigadoon:*

Because it was written in 1947, *Brigadoon's* "contemporary" scenes are actually post-World War II; however, they play just as well (and are easier to costume) in 1990s clothing. The Scottish scenes are mid-18th century.

Costume the village women in simple sashed dresses (ankle-length) made of pastel cotton; buckled shoes with splayed heels (fortunately, these are popular in the 1990s); long, decorative aprons; hair ribbons (younger women); mob caps (old women); and capes for evening scenes.

Dress the men in plain, dark trousers tucked into tall boots, which have turned-down tops just below the knee. (Tops can be made from lighter-color velour.) An alternative to boots is a pair of brown leather slippers with trousers tucked into the tops of drab "oversocks" (use warm-up socks). Pants *must* be fastened down — fold pant legs over at the ankles and secure with large rubber bands before tucking them into socks. Shirts are full-sleeved; and older men have plain, knee-length cloth coats, worn unbuttoned. Some older men wear hats with round crowns and flat brims. Work some soft, muted plaid into the overall scheme — one or two of the men's pants or a vest. Some of the men will need kilts. (Kilts cross over into *Finian's Rainbow,* Chapter 4.)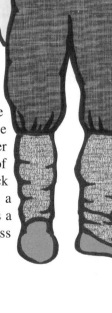

Jean's wedding dress: Ankle-length white or cream gown with same color sash and not a lot of fullness. (Make from a gauze-type material. Could also be made from old lace tablecloths or sheer curtains.) Headpiece is a long portion of the same material hanging loose over back and shoulders — held in place with a wreath of flowers (artificial). She carries a bouquet. Laurey's wedding dress

(*Oklahoma!*, Chapter 5) can be modified for Jean — remove some of the fullness at the shoulders and waist.

Fiddler on the Roof (*1905 Russia*)

Jerry Bock, Sheldon Harnick and Joseph Stein based their 1964 musical on stories by Sholom Aleichem.

This is Russia in 1905, where each person is a fiddler on the roof, "...trying to scratch out a pleasant, simple tune without breaking his neck." In other words, life here is dangerous, but it's home, and the Jewish villagers choose to cope with the persecution and stay. They draw their strength from "Tradition" (one of the show's best songs).

Tevye has three daughters who don't cooperate with his arrangements (of marriage) to ensure their safety and comfort. The girls want to be "in love," and Tevye can't understand what love has to do with marriage!

This homey storyline is played out against a backdrop of vandalism and the very real threat of eviction for all villagers. Eventually, Tevye takes what's left of his family and, sadly, leaves for America.

Costumes for *Fiddler on the Roof:*

Tevye wears a soft, collarless shirt with long sleeves (beige or moss green), a buttoned velour vest, soft cap, and dark loose pants tucked into low-heeled, midcalf boots.

His wife, Golde, wears an ankle-length skirt with clunky leather shoes; plain apron; a long-sleeved, plaid men's shirt (buttoned and worn as a jacket); and a babushka — a cotton kerchief tied under the chin.

Other characters are dressed similarly, in drab peasant costumes. All costumes should be weathered. Most men have beards.

Costumes from *Porgy and Bess* (Chapter 6) will cross over into this show.

Joseph and the Amazing Technicolor Dreamcoat (*Bible times*)

Written by Andrew Lloyd Webber and Tim Rice, *Joseph* first

appeared in 1968 (a twenty-minute version) but didn't open in New York until 1982 as a full-scale musical.

Joseph, an interpreter of dreams, is the favorite of the twelve sons of Jacob. To show his favoritism, Jacob gives Joseph a coat of many colors. This makes his brothers jealous — so jealous, in fact, that they sell Joseph to some merchants who take him to Egypt; then they tell their father that his favorite son is dead.

Through a chain of circumstances, Joseph meets Pharaoh and is asked to interpret a dream. Pharaoh is so impressed that he puts Joseph in charge of Egypt, second only to himself.

Meanwhile back at the farm, the brothers are having second thoughts. They travel to Egypt, but do not recognize Joseph (who has become very important over the past several years). Joseph, who certainly does recognize them, lets them humble themselves before him. Finally, he tells them who he is and says that he is not angry with them.

Joseph, dreaming of his beautiful coat and its significance, goes home to see his father, to "return to the beginning."

Costumes for *Joseph and the Amazing Technicolor Dreamcoat*:

Characters in this show dress like Bible-times characters, sort of. There is one major difference: The costumes are "stylized." In other words, a little on the weird side, like costumes in *The Wiz*.

Generally, Old-Testament men and women wore tunics (T-shaped, long shirts reaching almost to the ankles) with short or long sleeves and an over-garment, which was open down the front and had decorated borders. Hems of tunics were either plain or fringed.

The over-garment (various lengths) could have short, long or no sleeves; it also could be cape-style with slits for the arms; or, it could be a simple (but large-size) shawl. Cloth waistbands, tied in front, had decorated ends.

Long hair was the custom for both sexes, and many women braided theirs. Some women wore head coverings (long pieces of cloth hanging loose in back); men used headbands.

Now, imagine all that in bold prints...and with athletic socks and tennis shoes on the feet! Stretch the imagination even further —

picture a group of men in such ancient costumes, all made of various patterns in only black and white...or only red and gold...or only blue and silver. Get the idea?

Joseph's "technicolor dreamcoat" or his "coat of many colors" is his over-garment. Use wide, vertical stripes in as many bright colors as possible. His coat *must* stand out from the other actors' costumes. Trim it in gold or silver.

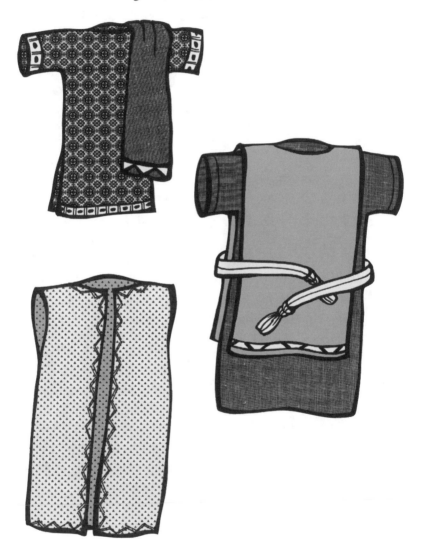

The King and I *(19th-century England and Siam)*

This 1951 Richard Rodgers and Oscar Hammerstein musical is based on Margaret Landon's novel, *Anna and the King of Siam*. It is a true story with no romance between the chief players.

The show's charm hinges on the meeting of two diverse cultures, when Anna Leonowens (with her young son) arrives in Siam in the 1860s as a teacher to the king's sixty-seven children.

The brusque king cannot help raising his internal antenna to Anna's strange ways. For one thing, he cannot dominate her as he does the women of his kingdom. Fascinating to watch is his furtive attention to Anna's lessons, and his gradual change in attitude: A barbaric, tantrum-throwing dictator ends (literally, his life) in tune with Anna's humane teachings.

Costumes for *The King and I*:

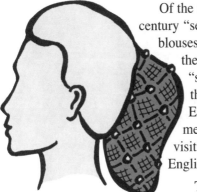

Of the major characters, Anna wears 19th-century "serviceable" dresses, long skirts and blouses, and a hoop-skirted ball gown. (If the performer has long hair, a jeweled "snood" would be fashionable with the gown.) Anna's son, too, wears English clothing — small versions of menswear; and Sir Edward Ramsey, a visiting diplomat, dresses in fashionable English attire (See Chapter 4).

The Siamese characters all wear shimmering, brilliantly colored, Oriental creations — loose pants and sleeves banded at wrists and ankles; ankle bracelets; bare feet or, for some characters, shoes with pointed, upturned toes (add "toes" to ballet slippers); small hats (pillbox-style but with rounded edges) or slim tall ones — both styles sit directly on top of the head; and trimmings of gilt and beads. An alternative (or additional) costume would be an ankle-length, straight-cut robe (coat) with a short stand-up collar. Robe is trimmed down the front and around the bottom and sleeves with gold braid. Choose an assortment of bright colors for the robes.

The ballroom scene is fun. The king wants to convince Sir Edward that his people are just as civilized as Europeans. So, he has Anna dress the women of the court in hoop-skirted gowns, which (unfortunately) flip up in back when they bow, embarrassing the king!

Hoop skirt: Hand-sew a Hula-Hoop (purchase in a toy store) into the bottom of a full petticoat.

The Music Man (*1912 America*)

Written by Meredith Willson, *The Music Man* took all awards of the 1957 season, edging out a tough competitor, *West Side Story*.

"Con man" Harold Hill arrives in River City, Iowa, planning to sell band instruments along with a promise to teach youngsters how to play. He also plans to collect the money and leave town before the instruments are delivered!

"Marian the Librarian," however, spots him as a swindler. With threat of exposure, she forces him to stay and make good on his promise of lessons. Trouble is, Harold Hill can't read music! Nevertheless, he prepares the band to play "Seventy-Six Trombones." The resultant sound is clatter of the worst sort but real music to the ears of townspeople and doting parents. Hill becomes a hero, not only to them but to Marian as well.

Costumes for *The Music Man:*

What fun this one is to costume! The chorus ends up in band uniforms. Many schools have old, discarded uniforms, boxed or hanging in an obscure closet. This would be the best choice. They could be trimmed or "de-trimmed" and altered as necessary. If the committee makes uniforms, choose simple cuts with simple trimming, so that they will look "homemade." Pants are baggy-cut; and hats should be the old-fashioned, tall ones with straight-up plumes (purchased in a craft shop).

Harold wears a brightly colored, double-breasted sport coat (buttoned) with shirt and bow tie; striped, cuffed trousers with sharp creases; and a straw "boater" hat. Townsmen dress similarly but not as flashy. Some wear loose short coats ("tweeds" with patch pockets) or no coat at all, and pleated trousers. Straw hats or felt bowlers are worn or carried by the men in all outdoor scenes. Leather shoes.

When Harold directs the band, either give him a band uniform (possibly in reverse colors) or dress him in all white with a bow tie the color of the uniforms.

Marian and the women wear ankle-length dresses or straight-cut skirts (no "flounces" or petticoats). Tops are fuller (bosoms were fashionable) and wrist-length sleeves are close-fitting. Out of doors, women wear large hats trimmed with ribbons or feathers. See *Hello, Dolly!* (Chapter 4) for crossover possibilities.

You're a Good Man, Charlie Brown (*Teens dressed as children*)

Writer Clark Gesner based this 1967 offering on the comic strip, *Peanuts*, by Charles Schulz. The small cast (eight members) is made up of teenagers who play the parts of six-year-old children. This show is lovable, upbeat and funny.

The loosely knit story looks at a day in the life of Charlie Brown and his friends. All familiar elements are there: The children needle Charlie by singing, "You could be king, if only you weren't so wishywashy." Lucy, naturally, wants to be queen and tell everyone what to do. There's Linus and his blanket, Snoopy and his eternal quest for the Red Baron and, of course, a baseball game. The finale is about "true happiness," which aptly sums up this musical.

Costumes for *You're a Good Man, Charlie Brown:*

The best way to costume this show is to collect several weeks of *Peanuts* from the "Sunday funnies." All of the comic strip characters still live and play there, in vivid color!

CHAPTER 10
In Your Dreams!

Every once in awhile a show comes along that fulfills a costumer's wildest dreams. The characters are wonderfully wacky, the storyline is colorful and imaginative, and the setting and music seem to spark creativity in unique ways — a show that's pure *joy* to costume!

Such costuming may be fairly easy *(A Chorus Line)* or complicated and time-consuming *(Barnum)*. But it will never be boring. Think of the fun in re-creating Little Boy Blue, Simple Simon, Bo Peep and other nursery-rhymers for *Babes in Toyland*; or the satisfaction of constructing a tin man for *The Wizard of Oz*; or the challenge of turning humans into felines for *Cats*.

Following are six shows, along with instructions for creating two fine costumes from each — just enough to get the imagination cranked up and the mental machinery running!

A Chorus Line

By Marvin Hamlisch, Edward Kleban, James Kirkwood and Nicholas Dante, 1975.

Oddly enough, *A Chorus Line* doesn't have a "chorus" of players. Rather, it is a series of eighteen vignettes — eighteen hopeful performers auditioning for only eight positions. It speaks to anyone who has ever applied for a job of any kind and waited nervously for a decision. That, in essence, is the story.

Each applicant is seen in a personal and vulnerable way. In the end, the chorus line is expanded so that everyone wins.

How to Make Spectacular *High-Steppers*! *(Two outfits)*

For the song, "I Hope I Get It," dress each girl in a choice of the following: leotard and tights with a scarf or belt at the waist; leotard and sweat pants; leotard and tights with a short wrap skirt;

T-shirt over leotard and tights — pull bottom of shirt to one side and knot it at the waist. Some will have a towel around the neck, and leg-warmers or heavy white socks. Ballet, dance or jazz shoes — no tennis shoes! Girls' hair should be in a ponytail or chignon or otherwise pulled back from the face.

Each boy wears a choice of the following: T-shirts or tank tops with sweat pants or shorts (bike-length pants can be worn underneath the shorts); fitted trousers and shirt with full, flowing long sleeves. Some will have a towel around the neck. Jazz shoes with heavy socks.

Now, *transform* these hopefuls into a spectacular chorus line for the song, "One." Give each girl a black tank-top leotard, black tuxedo shorts and coat with tails, red cummerbund, red bow tie, black sheer-to-waist pantyhose, and black dance shoes. Finish with a black top hat. No jewelry or nail polish.

Similarly, each boy wears black tuxedo pants and coat with tails, tux shirt, red cummerbund and bow tie, black shoes (the kind that lace) and black socks. Black top hat.

To keep tux shirts "tucked," attach a piece of ¼"-wide elastic to each shirt tail in front and sew the other ends to the sides of the shirt in back, going under the crotch area. Elastic should fit snugly to hold the shirt in place. Teenagers don't like this one bit. They'll complain and whine and beg; but be firm, because it is *absolutely necessary!*

If the top hat is too big, use a piece of thin foam (such as on hangers from a dry cleaning company, or an old foam ironing board cover). Cut ½" strips and hot glue them to the inside of the hat on the sides. Paint the foam black.

Babes in Toyland

By Victor Herbert and Glen MacDonough, 1903.

Two children survive a shipwreck, and find themselves stranded in Toyland with their wicked Uncle Barnaby. As they move through the Spider's forest, the palace of the Moth Queen, the Christmas Tree Grove and other magical places, they meet an assortment of Mother Goose characters.

Throughout their journey they are plagued by Barnaby and his tricks, but their new friends help outsmart him.

Finally, justice prevails in a Toyland court.

How to Make a Beautiful *Bo Peep*!

Little Bo Peep needs a light blue cotton dress with a full skirt (hemmed up 6" from the floor), petticoats and short puffy sleeves. Trim the sleeves with a ruffle of lace or eyelet. Give her a white apron that has a bib and ties in back with a big bow.

Bo also wears pantalets — long ruffled "drawers" that extend below the skirt. Under the pantalets are white tights, and on her feet are white or pink "Mary Jane" shoes. (To achieve the look of Mary Janes, cover an elastic band with cloth the same color as the little flat shoes and slip it over the foot, across and under the arch.)

Give her a "Shirley Temple" wig — plenty of curls in blond or brunette — and a blue bonnet with white ruffle. Bonnet is fitted over the ears and ties under the chin with ribbons.(See Sister Sarah's bonnet — *Guys and Dolls*, Chapter 6, but make the brim larger.) For Bo Peep's staff, use a cane with an extender.

How to Make a Triumphant *Toy Soldier*!

Dress this spiffy soldier in navy, white and red and gold. Choose a navy satin or rayon shirt with a high collar and long sleeves (look for a lady's blouse at the thrift shop); navy trousers and socks; dark shoes or plain, knee-high boots. Make two 4"-wide, white straps (use sturdy material) to crisscross over the shirt, front and back as shown, and stich them to the shoulders. Leave enough length so the straps can be pinned to the trousers after the performer has dressed.

Make epaulets from heavy cardboard, such as the top of a gift box. Cover with gold satin and sew gold fringe all around, except where the epaulet meets the collar. Sew in place.

Make the hat with poster board and cover it with red fake fur (use hot glue). The under-the-chin strap is white — an old belt or piece of vinyl. Finishing touches: a gold button at top of chin

116

strap on each side; gold tassel halfway up one side of hat. Be sure the hat sits down on the forehead.

Barnum

By Cy Coleman, Michael Stewart and Mark Bramble, 1980.

This is fiction, with Barnum (of circus fame) and his wife as the central figures. *Barnum's* appeal is not in the plot, which is broth-thin, but in the variety of colorful characters (every sort one would expect to see in a circus), the atmosphere created by the circus-like staging, the circus-type acts (juggling, clowning, etc.) and (yes!) the costumes.

How to Make a Tremendous *Two-Headed Lady*!

Cut the top *exxxxtra* large, since it has to fit two girls! Use stretch, polyester knit in a brightly colored print; cut and ruffle-trim two neck holes.

The gathered, full skirt (solid color) needs to be long, so that the feet do not show. (The girls must wear socks and/or shoes that are the same color as the skirt.) Put a waistband on the skirt, with placket in back.

Make a wide (6", doubled) nonstretch cloth belt, long enough to go around both girls, with a bow in the back to cover the placket.

Put identical bows in the girls' hair. Use bold colors.

The girls will have to stand shoulder to shoulder. If this becomes a problem (and it will!), tie their arms together with a strip of cloth.

How to Make a Towering *Tall Man*!

The first job is to teach the performer to walk on stilts! Great height is not important (this should make it easier), only that he rise above the other performers. For an alternative to stilts, make a pattern on the soles of the performer's shoes and cut several "soles" from wood. Nail them together in a stack (as shown on page 119) until the desired height is reached.

This fellow (or girl) wears a white tuxedo shirt or long-sleeved dress shirt with a navy and white, extra-large, polka-dot bow tie. Make a jumpsuit of red and white, vertical-striped polyester fabric, long enough to slip into — no zipper needed. Allow for the extra length of the stilts. Paint stilts (or stacks) white and put no-skid bottoms on them (purchase from shoe repair shop), since maneuvering on the stage will be a little more difficult than on the ground. Top with the tallest top hat available — cover it in the same, vertical-striped material as the jumpsuit. Put a wide, solid-color navy band around it.

Cats

By Andrew Lloyd Webber, from T. S. Eliot's *Old Possum's Book of Practical Cats*, 1982.

Everything about this musical is larger than life — the characters (people dressed as cats), the setting (a junk yard), and the plot (selecting one cat to be sent to heaven for rebirth). The chief players vying for this angelic opportunity are Grizabella, Gus and Macavity.

Cats is absolute fantasy, and that's what makes it work so well. For a little while, the audience escapes to another world, one far removed from the daily workplace.

NOTE: Since *Cats* is still meowing on Broadway, the rights for amateur production are not yet available. Keep an eye on it, though. This one is a real winner. For more information, see Appendix B.

How to Make a Colossal *Cat*!

The basic costume is leotard and tights in brown, black or tan and matching long gloves. Some cats' body suits may be splashed with white fabric paint to create the illusion of a cat's fur patterns.

Make a tunic from an old fur coat (go second-hand shopping) or from fake fur. Cut strips an inch wide on sleeves and bottom (up to bust line) and cut hems (sleeves and bottom) unevenly. The goal here is "grungy."

Buy cat ears from a costume shop; or cut them from felt or other stiff fabric — make small cones as shown, stuff with cotton pads, and sew onto a cloth-covered headband. Sprinkle dark sequins in the hair while hair spray is wet and they'll stick!

Smudge face with black or brown eye shadow; draw whiskers with eyebrow pencil or acrylic paint; use long, black false eyelashes.

Shoes can be black or brown soft house slippers or high heels, depending on the desired look — heels look great during a solo, such as "Memory," but wouldn't be worn during the rest of the show.

How to Make a Great *Garbage Can*!

In *Cats*, the oversized props are almost as important as the critters who prowl around them. These may or may not fall into the costumer's "purrrrview," but they're worth a look. Here goes one:

Start with a cardboard mattress box. Remove the top layer of cardboard — underneath is a ridged layer, which is just the thing for the "barrel" part of the huge can. Cut the ridged layer to the desired height. Cut a circle from a piece of plywood to form the base of the can. Wrap the ridged cardboard vertically around the base and staple it on. Staple and glue the long seam, too. From the discarded plain layer, make smooth bands for the top and bottom, as shown. Spray paint the "can" flat steel gray and add black marks and a few dents to make it look weathered. Hang a cat's tail from the top, or staple some "trash" at the rim, to appear as if the can is full.

The Fantasticks

By Harvey Schmidt and Tom Jones, 1960; based on Edmond Rostand's play, *Les Romanesques*. (This "little" show is the longest running, most frequently produced musical in the world!)

The Fantasticks is a fantasy about growing pains. The Girl (Luisa) and The Boy (Matt) are neighbors, and their fathers are good friends. To encourage their children to fall in love, the fathers (using reverse psychology) build a wall between their homes and pretend to be enemies. When this doesn't work, they hire a bandit (El Gallo) to stage a mock abduction of Luisa so that Matt can save her. But Luisa and Matt end up quarreling and run away — separately.

Later, disillusioned with "real life," they return home and discover love for themselves.

Special effects are achieved very simply by an imaginative character called the Old Actor.

How to Make an Interesting *Indian*!

Costumes for *The Fantasticks* are not realistic. *Fantasticks* is a fantasy, so the costumes are, well...fantastic. For example, Luisa (who is also called The Girl) does not dress like a modern young woman. She wears a simple sashed dress with matching tights, flat shoes, and a bow in her hair. The fathers, too, are caricatures — baggy pants, suspenders, wide ties. The Mute's costume is elfin in style; and one especially interesting character is called The Indian. This is his outlandish costume:

Loose-fitting, long thermal underwear — dye it red, pink or purple. Cut a waistband and two 12" squares from tan or yellow imitation suede or from an old piece of chamois. Sew the squares to the band as shown, one in front and one in back. He also wears a long black wig, divided into two braids, and a sweatband with one droopy feather attached.

How to Make a Marvelous *Mute*!

This one's easy — all black color, covering everything but the face and hands: long-sleeved turtleneck shirt, trousers, socks, soft vinyl slippers, top hat, gloves.

The Wizard of Oz *[and]* *The Wiz*

By L. Frank Baum.

The Wizard of Oz (adapted by Frank Gabrielson, with music and lyrics of the MGM motion picture score by Harold Arlen and E. Y. Harburg) sweeps Dorothy and her dog, Toto, out of Kansas and into Oz, via a tornado.

Dorothy and her new-found friends — Scarecrow, Tin Man and Lion — look for the Wizard, the only one who can send her back to Kansas. The Wizard's price: They must foil the "Wicked Witch of the West." Familiar songs are "Over the Rainbow," "We're Off to See the Wizard" and others. (Costume ideas for *The Wizard of Oz* can be found in the film, available on video.)

The story of *The Wiz* — an all-black interpretation of *The Wizard of Oz* — sticks very close to the movie version (and to Baum's original). The music by Charlie Smalls, however, is unrelated to either. It's flavor is "soul" and includes "Ease on Down the Road," which became a popular favorite. Costumes in the Broadway production were wild, colorful and very imaginative (make that *weird*) — and the "tornado" was represented by a dancer, whirling around in yards of dark, filmy cloth!

How to Make a Terrific *Tin Man*!

For *The Wizard of Oz*, the basic costume is sweat shirt and sweat pants in gray, white or cream; white or gray socks; white gloves; shoes or short boots without laces (all *old*).

For the vest, use a fabric with a sleek finish, or something heavy enough to spray paint silver. For length, measure the performer from shoulder to right below the tummy, double the measurement and allow for a small hem around the bottom. For width, measure around the chest and tummy and add a few inches. Fold piece in half, cut neck and arm holes.

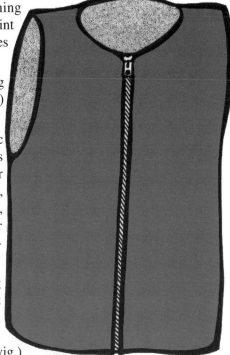

Spray paint everything silver. Use silver acrylic paint to make up the face. (It comes off easily.)

Put a blond curly wig and an inverted funnel (to fit) on the head.

For *The Wiz*, the basic tin man costume is a man's old, sleeveless fiber-filled or down vest, old trousers, light-colored sweat shirt, white gloves and socks or short boots. Spray everything with silver paint.

Use a black curly wig and an old aluminum skillet (with aluminum handle) on the head. (Sew or hot glue the skillet upside-down to wig.) Use silver acrylic paint to make up the face.

How to Make a Scrappy *Scarecrow*!

For *The Wizard of Oz*, use real straw and dress the performer just as scarecrows in the fields are/were dressed. (It's rare to see a real one these days!) Give him patched overalls, dull plaid shirt, dilapidated hat, and plenty of straw sticking out from everywhere, particularly from under the hat (anchor the straw with hot glue). Stuff his clothes with rags so that he looks puffy.

The scarecrow in *The Wiz* (shown on page 126) needs a bright plaid shirt and trousers in maroon and gold or red and yellow, and yellow crepe paper strips in place of straw. Give him a natural straw pillbox hat and sew or hot glue the strips around it to look like hair. Attach more strips to sleeve and trouser cuffs (make the pants "high-waters"). Stuff him to look puffy, as above, and add more yellow strips to look like they're sticking out from the front of his shirt and from a seam or two.

APPENDIX A
The Costume Committee's Best Buddies

Glue
Glue Gun
Tape
Colored Tape
Black Electrical Tape
Pins
Staples
Velcro Fasteners
Pipe Cleaners
Wire
Wire Twisties
Rope
String
Spray Paint
Felt-tipped Markers
Fabric Dye
Stencils
Appliques
Glitter
Brads
Sequins
Cotton Balls
Fringe
Feathers
Artificial Flowers
Ribbon

Aluminum Foil
Gold Foil
Foam Rubber
Vinyl
Upholstery Samples
Fabric Remnants
Felt
Fake Fur
Burlap Bags
Old Sheets
Old Bedspreads
Old Blankets
Old Curtains
Old Draperies
Old Tablecloths
Scarves
Headbands
Suspenders
Leotards
Tights
Ballet Slippers
Bedroom Slippers
Christmas Decorations
Halloween Accessories
Valentine Decorations

Music Licensing Agencies

Agency	Code
G. Schirmer, Inc. 20th Floor 257 Park Ave., South New York, NY 10010 Phone: 212-254-2100	GS
Music Theatre International 545 Eighth Ave. New York, NY 10018-4307 Phone: 212-868-6668	MTI
Rodgers & Hammerstein Theatre Library 1633 Broadway New York, NY 10019 Phone: 212-564-4000	R&H
Samuel French, Inc. 45 W. 25th St. New York, NY 10010-2751 Phone: 212-206-8125	SF
Tams-Witmark Music Library, Inc. 560 Lexington Ave. New York, NY 10022 Phone: 800-221-7196	TW
The Dramatic Publishing Company P.O. Box 129, 311 Washington St. Woodstock, IL 60098 Phone: 800-HIT-SHOW	DP

The Really Useful Group, Ltd.   RUG
19 Tower St.
London WC2 H9NS
England
Phone: 44-171-240-0880

Theatre Maximus   TM
1650 Broadway, Suite 601
New York, NY 10019
Phone: 212-765-5913
(for the musical, *Godspell*, only)

APPENDIX C
Index of Shows

Show	Agency
A Chorus Line	TW
A Connecticut Yankee	R&H
A Funny Thing Happened on the Way to the Forum	MTI
Ain't Misbehavin'	MTI
Amahl and the Night Visitors	GS
Annie	MTI
Annie Get Your Gun	R&H
Anything Goes	TW
Babes in Arms	R&H
Babes in Toyland	TW
Barnum	TW
Bells Are Ringing	TW
Brigadoon	TW
Bye Bye Birdie	TW
Cabaret	TW
Call Me Madam	MTI
Camelot	TW
Can-Can	TW
Carmen Jones	R&H
Carnival	TW
Carousel	R&H
Cats (Not yet available)	RUG

Damn Yankees	MTI
Dancin'	SO
Destry Rides Again	TW
Do Re Mi	TW
Dreamgirls	TW
Evita	MTI
Fiddler on the Roof	MTI
Finian's Rainbow	TW
Fiorello!	TW
Flower Drum Song	R&H
42nd Street	TW
Funny Girl	TW
Girl Crazy	TW
Godspell	TM
Good News!	TW
Grease	SF
Guys and Dolls	MTI
Gypsy	TW
Hello, Dolly!	TW
How to Succeed in Business Without Really Trying	MTI
I Can Get It for You Wholesale	TW
Joseph and the Amazing Technicolor Dreamcoat	MTI
Jumbo	R&H
Kismet	MTI
Kiss Me, Kate	TW

Stop the World — I Want to Get Off	TW
Strike Up the Band	MTI
The Boy Friend	MTI
The Boys from Syracuse	R&H
The Fantasticks	MTI
The King and I	R&H
The Merry Widow	TW
The Music Man	MTI
The Pajama Game	MTI
(The) Phantom (of the Opera) — Kopit-Yeston version	SF
The Phantom of the Opera — Robinette-Chauls version	DP
The Phantom of the Opera	
(Andrew Lloyd Webber version — not yet available)	RUG
The Sound of Music	R&H
The Student Prince	TW
The Unsinkable Molly Brown	MTI
The Wiz	SF
The Wizard of Oz	
(Music and lyrics from the MGM motion picture score)	TW
Timbuktu	MTI
Two Gentlemen of Verona	TW
West Side Story	MTI
Where's Charley?	MTI
Wildcat	TW
Wonderful Town	TW
You're a Good Man, Charlie Brown	TW

APPENDIX D
Index

139

Bibliography

Bordman, Gerald. *American Musical Theatre: A Chronicle*. 2nd ed. New York: Oxford University Press, 1992.

Gorsline, Douglas. *What People Wore: A Visual History of Dress From Ancient Times to Twentieth-Century America*. New York: Bonanza Books, 1952.

Green, Stanley. *Broadway Musicals, Show by Show*. Milwaukee, WI: Hal Leonard Books, 1985.

Jones, Tom, and Harvey Schmidt. *The Fantasticks, 30th Anniversary Edition*. New York: Applause Theatre Book Publishers, 1990.

Lerner, Alan Jay. *The Musical Theatre: A Celebration*. New York: McGraw-Hill Book Company, 1986.

Nunn, Joan. *Fashion in Costume, 1200-1980*. New York: Schocken Books, 1984.

Ross, Beverly B., and Jean P. Durgin. *Junior Broadway*. Jefferson, NC: McFarland & Company, Inc., Publishers, 1983.

Watson, Philip J. *Costume of Old Testament Peoples*. Edgemont, PA: Chelsea House Publishers, 1987.

Wilcox, R. Turner. *Five Centuries of American Costume*. New York: Macmillan Publishing Company, 1963.

About the Authors

Janet Litherland began her life-long romance with the arts as a five-year-old in a local theater, where she sang and danced to *God Bless America* — in a spiffy, red-white-and-blue costume.

After growing up, earning a degree in music from Indiana University of Pennsylvania, and studying at the Musical Theatre Academy in New York City, she performed in plays and musicals in stock, road shows and off-Broadway. She also crossed the Arctic Circle with the U.S.O. in *The Boy Friend*, playing to remote Air Force bases. Her performance repertoire includes *Brigadoon, The Music Man, Gypsy, Bye Bye Birdie, Show Boat, The Pajama Game, Carousel, Fiorello!, Finian's Rainbow* and others. She has directed many musicals for high school and community groups.

In the past several years she has turned to writing as a means of creative expression. She is a prize-winning playwright and the author of eight books, including *The Complete Banner Handbook* and *Absolutely Unforgettable Parties*. (Meriwether Publishing Ltd.)

Janet and her husband, Jerry, live in Florida.

Sue McAnally is costume designer and wardrobe chairman for the Thomasville (Georgia) Music and Drama Troupe, a regional performance group of 200 teenagers, including ninety-six dancers. She has served in this capacity since 1977, costuming the Troupe for big-audience performances, including Atlanta Falcons football games. She currently serves as the Troupe's associate choreographer.

For the past twelve years, her costumes have adorned the Thomasville High School Show Stoppers, winners of the 1993 "Royal Hawaiian Classic," a worldwide competition for high school show choirs. With this group, she has spent part of several summers attending theater workshops in New York City. In addition, she serves as consultant to other area schools for their productions.

Her costume-designing repertoire of musicals and plays includes *Barnum, Pippin, Grease, Amahl and the Night Visitors, A Member of the Wedding, Under Milkwood* and others.

Sue and her husband, Bob, are the parents of five children and grandparents of eight.

ORDER FORM

MERIWETHER PUBLISHING LTD.
P.O. BOX 7710
COLORADO SPRINGS, CO 80933
TELEPHONE: (719) 594-4422

Please send me the following books:

_____ **Broadway Costumes on a Budget #TT-B166** $14.95
by Janet Litherland and Sue McAnally
Big-time ideas for amateur producers

_____ **Elegantly Frugal Costumes #TT-B125** $12.95
by Shirley Dearing
A do-it-yourself costume maker's guide

_____ **Stagecraft I #TT-B116** $14.95
by William H. Lord
A complete guide to backstage work

_____ **Costuming the Christmas and Easter** $9.95
Play #TT-B180
by Alice M. Staeheli
How to costume any religious play

_____ **Stage Lighting in the Boondocks #TT-B141** $10.95
by James Hull Miller
A simplified guide to stage lighting

_____ **Self-Supporting Scenery #TT-B105** $14.95
by James Hull Miller
A scenic workbook for the open stage

_____ **The Theatre and You #TT-B115** $14.95
by Marsh Cassady
An introductory text on all aspects of theatre

These and other fine Meriwether Publishing books are available at
your local bookstore or direct from the publisher. Use the handy
order form on this page.

NAME: _____

ORGANIZATION NAME: _____

ADDRESS: _____

CITY:_____ STATE: _____ ZIP: _____

PHONE: _____
❏ **Check Enclosed**
❏ **Visa or MasterCard #** _____

Signature: _____   *Expiration*
Date: _____
(required for Visa/MasterCard orders)

COLORADO RESIDENTS: Please add 3% sales tax.
SHIPPING: Include $2.75 for the first book and 50¢ for each additional book ordered.

❏ *Please send me a copy of your complete catalog of books and plays.*

ORDER FORM

MERIWETHER PUBLISHING LTD.
P.O. BOX 7710
COLORADO SPRINGS, CO 80933
TELEPHONE: (719) 594-4422

Please send me the following books:

_____ **Broadway Costumes on a Budget #TT-B166** $14.95
by Janet Litherland and Sue McAnally
Big-time ideas for amateur producers

_____ **Elegantly Frugal Costumes #TT-B125** $12.95
by Shirley Dearing
A do-it-yourself costume maker's guide

_____ **Stagecraft I #TT-B116** $14.95
by William H. Lord
A complete guide to backstage work

_____ **Costuming the Christmas and Easter** $9.95
Play #TT-B180
by Alice M. Staeheli
How to costume any religious play

_____ **Stage Lighting in the Boondocks #TT-B141** $10.95
by James Hull Miller
A simplified guide to stage lighting

_____ **Self-Supporting Scenery #TT-B105** $14.95
by James Hull Miller
A scenic workbook for the open stage

_____ **The Theatre and You #TT-B115** $14.95
by Marsh Cassady
An introductory text on all aspects of theatre

These and other fine Meriwether Publishing books are available at
your local bookstore or direct from the publisher. Use the handy
order form on this page.

NAME: _____

ORGANIZATION NAME: _____

ADDRESS: _____

CITY:_____ STATE: _____ ZIP: _____

PHONE: _____
  ❏ **Check Enclosed**
  ❏ **Visa or MasterCard #** _____

Expiration
Signature: _____ *Date:* _____
    (required for Visa/MasterCard orders)

COLORADO RESIDENTS: Please add 3% sales tax.
SHIPPING: Include $2.75 for the first book and 50¢ for each additional book ordered.

  ❏ *Please send me a copy of your complete catalog of books and plays.*